Someone's Done Something Wrong

Revenge, Hatred and Humility

John E Waterston

Copyright © 2017 John E Waterston
All rights reserved.
ISBN-13:978-1533361073

For Jochen and Bernd
love and gratitude

CONTENTS

PREFACE	i
If we cannot save anything else, we can save face	1
It's easier to fall out of love than out of hate	16
Man that studieth revenge keeps his own wounds green	31
The sweetest kind of drunkenness	43
The greatest invention in the history of life	60
Self-consciousness begets self-importance begets anxiety	77
Seeking what is true is not seeking what is desirable	91
The endless struggle to think well of themselves	103
A lazy kind of grieving	120
Turn your grievance into grieving…	138
…and let them get away with it	156
NOTES AND FURTHER READING	167
BIBLIOGRAPHY	182
INDEX	185

PREFACE

When we feel bad, most of us have a tendency to adopt the belief that someone's done something wrong. This tendency is as commonplace as it is psychologically disingenuous and emotionally futile. There is little doubt that people are capable of doing very wrong things and such things can make others feel bad. This book is not about right and wrong, or the good and bad actions that we are all capable of and surrounded by every day. It is an exploration of the bad feelings that arise as a consequence of people's actions and how we might find non-injurious and sustainable remedies for such feelings. It is about discovering remedies for the emotional residue of feeling wronged, feeling injured, hurt or betrayed by others. I will suggest throughout that to focus on the wrong or the wrongdoer does very little to soothe the distressing and tenacious internal emotional consequences of our widespread human capacity for violence, exploitation and abuse towards ourselves and others.

It might be that we've done something wrong, or that someone else has done so, but in either case the assumption is often made: bad feelings spring from bad deeds and therefore the remedy for the bad feeling lies in the sphere of the bad deed. A quick look at a daily newspaper on any day of the week will show us that this belief is widely held. Newspapers that are full of outraged stories concerning how bad some people have been, of how they are wrong, and how they are to be vilified, shunned and rightfully punished. There is almost no comment on how it actually feels to be wronged other than strident calls to pay people back for what they have done. Bad deeds result in bad, often unbearable, feelings and furthermore, feelings that people often never fully recover from. It appears to me to be perfectly reasonable to make these connections and then to develop ethical structures, such as the legislature and the executive of the law, in an attempt both to comfort the bad feelings, provide for reparation and to prevent the bad deeds from recurring.

The law, along with consensual ethical imperatives to good behaviour, is designed to protect us from physical harm and loss and also, from emotional distress such as fear and grief. Therefore, as a culture, we have established some structural safeguards against those bad feelings that are a direct result of bad deeds and this goes some way to resolve the problem of the emotional and psychological anguish we can impose on each other as a result of our behaviour. Nevertheless, personal experience also teaches us that however much the law or other norms of good behaviour might censure, disapprove, punish or demand reparation from the wrongdoer, substantial residues of bad feeling often remain. These emotional residues may leave the victim with an overwhelming feeling that justice has only partially been carried out, or not been done at all, and someone has still done something wrong and got away with it.

This book is an exploration of such emotional residues and how they develop within us. Also, the reasons for their astonishing tenacity and the ways that we might respond to them; effective, not so effective and hopelessly futile. More specifically, it is about the most common, highly developed and complex method we have of trying to deal with these residues of bad feeling – the creation of the revenge scenario. In my terms, the revenge scenario comprises the constellation of characteristic thoughts, emotions and behaviours that are aimed exclusively at not allowing someone to get away with what they have done by paying them back for what they have done.

In the following chapters I will be examining in detail the various elements of the revenge scenario and demonstrate how and where it fits into human psychological and emotional processes. I will reveal the function of the revenge scenario as a self-soothing mechanism and explain the reasons for its ultimate failure as a sustainable and reliable remedy for the hurts we endure. I will also propose objections to the continued use of revenge as a response to injury, not from a moral or ethical viewpoint but, from the point of view of a psychotherapist who has witnessed the mutually destructive circularity of this most human behaviour many times. Throughout 25 years of clinical practice, I have reached an understanding of the psychological and emotional mechanisms of revenge and can propose alternative and less destructive remedies for the staggering and very personal injuries we are all too willing to inflict on each other. My contention throughout is that revenge is to be dismissed as a viable remedy not because it is ethically wrong but because it does not work.

I have structured the book quite intentionally so that it echoes the psychotherapeutic process between therapist and client. Beginning with the simple and familiar I have then progressed to what is complex and not so familiar. I have tried to keep psychotherapeutic theory and language to a minimum but where this has seemed helpful, or unavoidable, I have included brief explanations or made references in the notes and further reading section at the back of the book. Additionally, I have also quite consciously used repetition of ideas and with each repetition explained a little more of my meaning in order to deepen understanding. Hence, the book builds upon itself and is intended to be read as a whole. My personal experience has shown me that these techniques, simple to complex and repetition to depth, serve well in psychological and emotional explorations where we are trying to clarify and master an intellectual conundrum, encourage flexibility and spaciousness in emotional response and invite a change in the way we live our lives.

My intention with this book is something similar and I expect it will be of interest to anyone who is challenged to find creative and life affirming ways to approach and soothe the truly awful and all too human feelings that inevitably follow in the wake of feeling wronged, hurt, betrayed, angered and disappointed by those around us.

CHAPTER ONE

If we cannot save anything else, we can save face

Tolstoy's[1] novel, 'Anna Karenina' begins with a reflection on unhappy families: 'Happy families are all alike; every unhappy family is unhappy in its own way.' By way of introducing my subject I want to describe a family, a fictional family, made up of elements taken from some of the actual families I have worked with over the years. My fictional family was a frantically unhappy family and I want to begin by describing the family and the manner in which it was 'unhappy in its own way'.

The first thing to be described about this family, as is common in many unhappy families, is the breakdown of the parent's marriage, separation and acrimonious divorce. This was rapidly followed by an almost complete absence of the father from the children's lives, other than short access visits and annual holidays. The marriage had shown signs of difficulties following the birth of the first child and, 4 years later and 6 months after the birth of the second child, the husband confessed an affair and announced his intention to leave. In his distress, and perhaps shame, he left almost immediately and refused to participate in an emotional winding-down or goodbyes, either with his wife or his children. One day he was there, the next day he was not. Like many fathers who leave their families, for one reason or the other, he quickly made himself more and more absent and set up an entirely new way of life that scarcely involved his children. As would be expected, their father's leaving was quite unbearable for the children and they struggled to cope with feelings of confusion, heartbreak, loss and helplessness. As is so often the case, they were also burdened with feelings of shame and guilt because they felt that somehow, it must be their fault. Why else would Daddy leave, except that there was something terribly wrong with us? Faced with overwhelming helplessness, the children quickly seized responsibility and shouldered the blame in the hope that, if they were accountable for him leaving, they could bring him back.

In trying to make sense of what had just happened to them the young children faced an unendurable emotional dilemma. Should they hate Daddy now like Mummy seems to do? Can they bear to miss him; is he now a good or a bad Daddy? If we are angry will he go away even more; how can we love him when he doesn't love us? What did we do wrong? These very young children were faced with an exceptionally dreadful experience and overwhelming feelings that they simply could not tolerate nor digest. So too for the mother and ex-wife struggling with equally unbearable feelings of loss and abandonment, together with colossal anxiety about how she might cope with the young children on her own. She found herself to be bereft of support and comfort and wholly mortified and humiliated by being so rejected. How could she possibly bear the children's distress when she had so much of her own?

The triple combination of grief, humiliation and powerlessness is almost impossible for anyone to bear for long and for this woman with two young children to care for, utterly unmanageable. Such feelings, when unchecked, are disabling to the body, destabilising to the mind and generate isolation and depression. Not only are they painful and belittling, many people become highly anxious in their wake and fear loss of control and breakdown. In addition, the mother discovered that this particular trio of emotions: grief, humiliation and powerlessness, were not well tolerated and supported in her family or, indeed, generally in her culture. Instead, she was expected to take a pill, keep busy or 'get over it' in a relatively short space of time. She was encouraged to move on and think of other things. It seemed no-one wanted these feelings around for long. How easy is it to sit with your best friend while they go through overwhelming loss, humiliation and powerlessness? Who can bear for long to sit with a child in the same state? Not easy for anyone.

On the other hand, when there's so much anxiety, heartache and despair around then surely, someone's done something wrong? How much easier is it to sit with a best friend, or a child, who is feeling angry and accusing? Might not it be more bearable for all concerned to feel angry, even hateful and vengeful? Rather this than the awful powerless, impotent feelings of being left behind unloved, unwanted and ashamed of yourself for not being good enough to make them stay.

In principle, there is an element of choice in emotional responses although, in practice, these choices are made very early in life. They develop through trial and error, discovering what works best and through learning from the people around you, discovering what seems to work in the particular family or situation we find ourselves in. For example, if my parents characteristically deal with disappointment by shouting and raging at the world it is highly likely either, that this will be my preference or, that I might do the opposite. In any event, my emotional response will be 'chosen' with reference to that of my parents or others in early childhood. My choice will be based upon what seems to work and what appears to maintain functional relationships. In the family I am describing therefore, it might be helpful to take a look briefly at the choices available to them in their awful predicament.

Both sets of grandparents had suffered combinations of brutal, and brutalising, parental abandonment, parental marital breakdown and as adults had experienced their own marital discontent and breakdown. Both maternal and paternal grandfathers of the children were disappointed and humiliated men, intensely competitive, grandiose and dismissive of others. The only surviving grandmother was tormented with anxiety, very poor self-esteem and yet was also quietly bitter and cynical, passively contemptuous of others. Progressing through the generations, here was a grief stricken family with repeated experiences of discontent, conflict in the home, abandonment and emotional desolation. Terrible experiences that had led firstly to feelings of humiliation and powerlessness and secondly, to anger and bitterness. No-where in this family was there any comfort for the true awfulness of these experiences other than a trip to the doctor for pills or by generating a venomous tirade against those who had done so much wrong. The defining behavioural motif, which endured through the generations, was the maintenance of hateful relationships wherein one person would refuse to speak to the other in an act of passive revenge. This was triggered by some real or imagined insult and could be maintained for many years, sometimes decades. Brother would not speak to brother nor to sister, son would not speak to mother nor to father, ex-wife would not speak to ex-husband. This behaviour endured and was always believed (by both parties) to be a completely justified and reasonable reaction. An intimately attached standoff, each waiting for the other to put right what they had done wrong. The sense of each and everybody being wronged by the other and rightfully owed reparation and vindication in their various grievances was firmly fixed in the family's behavioural and attitudinal character. So firmly fixed that it was almost impossible to consider any other response, emotional or behavioural. No-one could make the first move as this was felt to be an unendurable loss of face and plunge the person into the underlying unendurable feelings. Better to stay angry than descend into powerlessness and grief. On one occasion, a daughter refused the dying wish of her mother that she visit and did not attend the subsequent funeral. The immeasurable and palpable grief and regret being held at bay by violent outpourings of bitter accusation, historical grievance and hateful resentment.

Thus, following the latest marital breakdown and departure of the father and husband the family we are concerned with were pre-programmed by previous generations to respond in a characteristic way. What did indeed emerge was a combination of depressive anxiety, within which was a barely veiled accusation of being terribly wronged, and covert but raging desires to 'pay him back' for the betrayal that had been visited upon the family. The fact that he appeared to be happy and successful in his new life, with his new partner, made the feeling that he was getting away with something unendurable. The children had a slightly more difficult psychological manoeuvre[2] to make as there remained a dependency need to think of their father as a good man and not to direct their venom at him. In their mind, to be angry with him was particularly frightening and unthinkable as he had already shown that he was willing to leave if not adequately loved by them. He may well leave completely and forever if they showed him all their true feelings. This was, in practice, fairly easily solved as one of the characteristics of any revengeful manoeuvre is that it is perfectly possible to direct it elsewhere and a substitute person or situation will do just as well. A substitute, someone who is perceived to have committed some similar wrongdoing can act as stand-in for the father thereby protecting the father, adequately discharging the venom and keeping the grief and humiliation at bay. As we will see later, arriving on the scene within a few months of the breakdown, the step-father was a perfect stand-in. As he came to sit in the father's seat at the family table he became the ideal recipient of the hatred that rightly belonged to the father yet could not be consciously given to the father. The role of the scapegoat is to protect essential relationships whilst providing an outlet for the energy of revenge scenario in a safe way. An unhappy family, unhappy in its own way.

When I met this family the manoeuvres described above had coalesced into a more chronic and pervasive means of dealing with all manner of bad feelings. Almost all distressing feelings, especially feelings concerning vulnerability or powerlessness, were never experienced directly for very long, if at all. Whenever unhappiness of any kind was around, frustration about things not being how they wanted them to be, or people not doing what was wanted, the family automatically resorted to a characteristic emotional manoeuvre that brought some relief. Generation of hatred was the favoured and essential tool for protecting against the deeper, unendurable feelings. Hatred held the family together at times when it might otherwise fall apart. The manoeuvre was akin to a reflex in that the necessity to defend against vulnerability, humiliation and powerlessness was so immediate that it was not felt as a choice but as a right and proper response, wholly justified and correct. This manoeuvre I have come to call: 'Someone's Done Something Wrong'. The private logic, if it can be so called, argues that if we are feeling bad then someone's done something wrong. If we can find that person, or someone like that person, take revenge on them or make them put it right then, the bad feelings will go away.

I will show throughout this book that although this argument undoubtedly has appeal, if we track its rationale to its psychological and emotional core, we will find that it does not work. Firstly, because when we feel bad nobody usually feels themselves to have done anything wrong and therefore 'putting it right' will inevitably involve further feelings of being wronged elsewhere and hence, the alarming possibility that what we have done in seeking reparation will be returned to us later. Secondly, and more significantly, it does not work because the desire to avoid the triple demons of powerlessness, humiliation and loss itself reflects a deeper, pre-existing and much more serious emotional vulnerability that manoeuvring into the position of 'Someone's Done Something Wrong' does little or nothing to address.

However, this family were pre-programmed and seduced by the simple logic that anger replaces grief and powerlessness. Furthermore, that anger and accusation will be tolerated, supported and encouraged within the family and thereby salvage the family from disaster. There is ready emotional comfort arising from the capacity of righteous anger and hatred to transform unendurable feelings into other feelings that can be borne and supported by those around us. Furthermore, the promise of the revenge scenario includes transferring the bad feelings from ourselves to the wrongdoer. Revenge promises that we can make them feel the way we feel. Transferring the unendurable feeling state out and away from ourselves is a promise not to be passed up. This is a very primitive psychological protective manoeuvre and essentially results in the bad feelings being 'about' someone else, and therefore no longer about me. I will write much more later about how I think this manoeuvre is achieved but, for the time being, it's enough to see that feeling bad inside yourself, feeling lost or sad or heartbroken or like you're falling apart, can be made to appear to belong to someone else and comfort can be gained from this.

For example, if I feel disappointed in someone, or they behave like they don't care about me, this might make me feel alone and sad. Not nice feelings for anyone to experience and I am likely to seek out some way of comforting myself. I might, for example, tell myself that I am better off without them or, that I didn't really want what they had to offer or, I might simply rage at their betrayal. If I can find a way of believing that they have wronged me, I might feel justified in 'paying them back' in some way and thereby getting them to feel the way I feel. I might indeed discover that rage at an imagined wrongdoer is very helpful in coping with sadness and loneliness. In the family I have mentioned, feelings like loneliness or sadness were not feelings that anyone could really bear so nobody tolerated them for long. There was no comfort available for such feelings and no-one could endure them in themselves or in each other. There was no ability within the family for bearing and digesting such feelings consequently, they could only be crushed or spat out. For at least three generations, the culture of this family had been that feelings of grief and powerlessness were so frightening in their intensity, so threatening to the stability of the self and of the family, that they were to be avoided at any cost. In effect they had become taboo for this family.

The result was that any natural and ordinary feelings of loneliness and sadness, powerlessness or humiliation would, like a reflex, jump into a thought and this thought would be that 'someone's done something wrong'. In this way they could explain the feeling and imagine a remedy (putting the wrongdoer right). Even the more benign thought that *something's wrong* for me to be feeling like is translated into the dangerously malignant: *someone's wrong*. This I would call a 'psychological manoeuvre[2]' and was this particular family's habitual way of protecting themselves from some very difficult feelings and generating less problematic ones. The less difficult feeling in would be some flavour of accusing anger.

I saw over and over again in this family that generating accusing anger was helpful in maintaining emotional and psychological stability and holding them together – the fear being that they might otherwise fall apart. The awful fear that we might fall apart if we don't stay angry maintained and unhappy stability. Anger, and particularly the flavour of anger that is hatred, can be enormously comforting to a fragile emotional state. For the family threesome, mother and children, there was the added advantage of bonding in a pact of mutually comforting victimhood as the wrongdoer was almost always an outsider to the little group. In addition, the manoeuvre also protected them from each other and on the rare occasions that they did turn against each other it appeared to be at times when no outsider was readily available. On their isolated desert island of powerlessness, humiliation and grief, these were very dangerous times for the three of them and cordiality was usually re-established once a suitable external wrongdoer had been successfully identified. Anger, especially anger against someone, has boundaries and edges that can be pushed against. Loss, grief and sadness can feel much more like melting, falling, disintegrating and therein lies the threat accompanying such feelings. The generation of hatred can initiate a sense of being a contained and stable unit in a way that would be threatened by experiences of overwhelming powerlessness and grief.

It is very common for psychological manoeuvres to use this trick: an unbearable feeling is transformed by a thinking process that can generate a different, more bearable feeling. If we can think of feelings as being experienced in the body and thoughts in the head, it might be clearer how this works. Bad feelings reside in the body as sensation and our attention may be pulled towards thinking in order to move away from those bad feelings. If we can then think of a new interpretation of what's just happened we may be able to produce a new, and hopefully less bad feeling in the body. The unbearable feeling will then, in all likelihood, be lost under the new one. This can happen so fast that most of the time, we may not be aware of the first bad feeling. We don't feel lonely and sad, we just feel angry and accusing. Again, angry and accusing might be preferable to lonely and sad, especially if it keeps us in accord with the rest of the family and gives generates the idea that we can then do something to make ourselves feel better. In this family feeling lonely, sad and powerless is imagined to be so much more difficult to make better than feeling angry and accusing. All they had to do was put right the thing that someone's done wrong, to make it fair perhaps by getting justice or revenge or just to receive empathic understanding. Perhaps by continual accusation we might even get the wrongdoer to see that they've done something wrong, stop doing it and make good the harm they have done. Indeed, chronic misery, unhappiness and accusing bitterness, however expressed, is often a way of life that becomes a monument to the wrongs we feel ourselves to have suffered. A monument that we hope (usually in vain) one day will be noticed, honoured and reparations made.

Ultimately, the terrible tragedy for this family was that, over time, they developed a strong need to perpetually be angry and blaming. Indeed, one of the other things about the family, which was very obvious to anyone who came into contact with them for any length of time, was that their awful emotional struggles resulted in them being a chronically vengeful group of people. They continually contrived between themselves to construct and maintain of a degree of revengefulness that was both relentless in its tenacity and violent in its execution. As a consequence they had become isolated and rejected by many people, both in the wider family and outside it, who felt themselves to be unjustly accused and vilified. The Shakespearian nature of the tragedy reveals itself in that the awfulness of the original abandonment and the desperate emotional manoeuvres employed to soothe an intolerable situation only generated further abandonment. This feature is, of course, the central enduring motif of the revenge tragedy. This family's feelings of anger at being wronged, together with their absolute need not to feel sad, lonely and powerless, made the generation of revengeful hatred towards almost anybody who wasn't the same as them, or a part of them, an essential part of their armoury. As the emotional need to avoid certain feelings became entrenched, the necessary anger and hatred at perceived wrongdoers built remorselessly into a full-blown revenge scenario. The irresistible and unstoppable desire to 'pay them back' one day and thereby redeem the awfulness of their feelings, generated a furnace-like alchemical energy that coalesced and reinforced the defensive manoeuvre into an impenetrable emotional bastion. Like topping up a reservoir of hatred as it seeped away each day, the family would actively and continually seek out reasons to be further angered, and to seek out wrongdoers. The reservoir needed to be re-filled daily to prevent the emergence of powerlessness, humiliation and grief which, like some lost and sunken village, threatened to be exposed to conscious feeling experience. Predictably, a rare happy event was almost always swiftly followed by days of spoiling, hectoring, arguing and scapegoating in order to re-establish the crushing of the softer, dangerous feelings.

Revenge is an irrational act inasmuch as it is driven by emotional, rather than cognitive needs and desires. It is a manoeuvre designed primarily to protect ourselves from psychological pain. The revenge manoeuvre is possibly the most favoured of all human defences and is the final result of a psychological and emotional cascade initiated by a simple need not to experience certain feelings. The tipping point is provided by emotional distress related to helplessness, humiliation and loss and, once begun, is impelled by defensive emotional imperatives down an uncomfortable but increasingly promising cascade. The promise is hard to resist and is nothing less than liberation from anguish for ourselves and suffering for those who have wronged us. The phenomenon of revenge might be seen as the most enduring feature of human relationships throughout history. It stands at the pinnacle of the manoeuvre described herein – that someone's done something wrong.

Two well understood features of emotions that are denied or pushed away is firstly, that they do not go away and secondly, that they push back. If, to take our example, there is a pushing away of feelings related to loss and grief (in this instance, replaced by anger) then those feelings do not simply go away. They do appear to go away, in that we stop being aware of them, yet they remain waiting and pushing for expression, to be vented at another time. This is similar to holding down a spring. It takes constant strength and energy to keep the spring down and it's always threatening to bounce up again. Many people will recognise the upward pressure as we often react to all kinds of emotional stimulation by pushing the feelings away, downward back to the body.

With our fictional family the spring, being composed of the feelings of loss and grief, was held down by thoughts of wrongdoing and feelings of anger towards the wrongdoer. As we have already seen, anger gets more support and comfort in some families than do powerlessness and grief. The cultural support will be to maintain as much pressure on the spring as is necessary to keep it down and not allow it to be expressed, or even consciously felt. My experience is that feelings like powerlessness, humiliation and grief are very commonly suppressed in this way and that such a repressive force is culturally encouraged. Our culture, our families, will spontaneously and unthinkingly collude to keep the 'spring' well and truly compressed. I will need to stay angry, you will help me to stay angry and even keep looking for things to make me angry, in order to keep the forces of powerlessness, humiliation and grief exactly where we need them to be. The unspoken social contract states: we all know that the alternative to anger and outrage is unbearably humiliating and a wholly unacceptable outpouring of loss and grief so, let's stay angry together.

The family in our example are doing nothing wrong. They are simply doing what seems to work within their culture and that great harm and misery stems from this does not make it wrong. It makes it tragic. The family in our example are in a kind of psychological and emotional cultural trap within which their cognitive and behavioural options are severely limited. They are caught by the need to stay angry and accusing in order to keep pressure on the ever hazardous spring that would otherwise release powerlessness and grief.

Tragically, the suppression of grief and shame also prevents any possibility of lasting resolution of the deeper emotional need. If we might assume an alternate reality for a moment, a different kind of family, a possibility could be that if the underlying grief and shame were allowed expression in a safe and reliable way there may be less need to generate hatred. However, within the rigid confines of the trap that is the revenge scenario, any comfort that might be available and expressed in kindness towards grief and the shame, will likely be met with an onslaught of anger, whose sole purpose is to keep the spring well and truly compressed. Anyone who, in kindness and with good intention, has approached an unhappy and sulking adolescent will know this well and probably bear the scars.

One of the interesting things about feeling wronged is that it is entirely possible to feel desperately wronged even though no wrongdoing has taken place. The phrase 'the law is an ass', popularised by Mr Bumble[3] in Oliver Twist, is one such example of this. We might use this phrase when we feel wronged by people who are acting perfectly legitimately within the law. Indeed, the kind of wrongdoing that brings clients to my consulting room is generally of this kind. Generally, no offense in law has been committed and yet the person feels terribly wronged, hurt and angry and cannot settle until this is attended to in some way to their satisfaction. In the case of the family mentioned previously, no offense has been committed, no prosecution could be brought and yet, the feeling of being mortally wronged remains. Even as I type this last sentence, I feel the impulse to quarrel is enormous – surely someone has done something wrong? Is it possible for such appalling feelings to exist, such terrible suffering to be created, in the absence of wrongdoing?

It may well be that someone has done something wrong but I would argue that to pursue this in the hope of making the bad feelings go away is a circular, and ultimately fruitless, excursion. As I have described, the necessity to maintain anger and vengefulness and avoid powerlessness, humiliation and grief will remain precariously balanced on the edge of an enduring anxiety that will forever threaten to topple and fall into frenzied chaos and overwhelming distress. Not only will it remain as a perilous equilibrium, it will also come to serve as a keystone upon which the whole of a person's psychological and emotional comfort relies. It is likely to constitute one of the central motifs in any current or future personal relationship and produce predictably destructive consequences. Evolving into an amorphous, but vital, necessity for psychological stability we simply cannot let them get away with it. This inability to let them get away with it commonly threatens to overspill and poison every future relationship a revengeful person will engage in.

Two years after the end of my involvement with the family I was asked for a consultation with the man who had stepped into the role of second husband and step-father. He began by telling me that he had withdrawn from the household and the marriage. I was aware from our previous meeting that he had entered the marriage feeling blessed, in love and optimistic for the future. In testament to the power of the revenge scenario to transfer unbearable states of mind from one person to another, he spoke of feeling overwhelmed by failure, humiliated, betrayed and heartbroken. Six months after leaving the household he was still being assaulted by abusive and threatening messages from the two step-children.

He spoke openly about his own revengeful behaviour within the family and was shamed by this. However, he also spoke of the pleasure he gained from surreptitiously damaging the household and felt justified in his actions. Undoubtedly, he had also acted out his own revenge scenario as he encountered his own naivety and feelings of being wronged and powerless within the family. In coming to sit in the absent father's seat he was unknowingly setting up an impossibly complex and ultimately futile attempt at restoration. Perhaps his own grandiosity in believing that this would have a happy ending made him culpable too but what remained for all was a desperate powerless misery stemming from the tenacity of a trans-generational emotional need to not feel something believed to be unendurable. In an even more chilling twist he revealed that he too was still comforted in his current distress by thoughts of revenge.

There's an old joke I have always liked because it somehow points to the dilemma we are facing when dealing with wrongs and wrongdoing. It goes like this: a man finds himself in a strange town and is asking a passer-by for directions to the railway station. The passer-by thinks for a moment and eventually says, 'well, I really wouldn't start from here…' My contention in the following pages is similar. I wouldn't start in the obvious place, with the wrong and the wrongdoer. My experience is that the less obvious place to start is far harder to find but it might get us where we want to go less injuriously and in a more emotionally sustainable way.

The fictional family I mention are not unique and their story by no means unusual. The need to receive comfort and to comfort ourselves in the face of such devastating experiences is beyond question. The transformation of dangerously destabilising feelings (grief, humiliation and powerlessness) into emotional reactions that might reduce this danger (anger, hatred and impulses to revenge) is wholly understandable and, in some ways, to be supported. It is indisputable that people do terrible things, things which are rightly viewed as 'wrong', and there are social and community remedies for some of these things. Such remedies belong to the realm of justice, perhaps the law, and involve ethics and thoughts of rightful and fair punishment or reparation. This book is not about these aspects of wrongdoing. This book is an examination of the emotional and psychological processes that are activated when we feel wronged.

My work over the years has brought me into contact with many people who feel wronged in one way or the other. People who have been betrayed, suffered violence, been brutally ignored, been sadistically manipulated, been overpowered and abused and tortured. They have been left with feelings of outrage, impotence, humiliation, self-loathing, loneliness and overwhelming sadness. Common to all these people is a tenaciously held belief that someone, somewhere, has got away with something and this is unendurable to them. Indeed, some are so consumed by thoughts and feelings that 'they've got away with it', they cannot attend to any of life's other demands until this situation is resolved. With some individuals I have met, the belief and the feelings that go along with it are so extreme they consume the sufferer's conscious awareness to the exclusion of all else. For such people, to let the wrongdoer get away with it is so unthinkable, and emotionally unbearable, so much a betrayal of themselves, their honour and self-esteem that they will pursue the wrongdoing, and the wrongdoer as a life's work.

I am aware of how easily we might get seduced into believing that when we feel wronged the remedy for our emotional distress lies chiefly in identifying, exposing and punishing the wrongdoing. Like any addictive illusion it does feel like this is the right solution and that it will work for us. In some ways it is right and it does work. However, in psychological and emotional terms it can be seen that it is not right and it doesn't work. To give up on the revenge scenario, something that so nearly works, is desperately difficult. We may even find that the pursuit of ethically proscribed justice often does little to change our experience of ourselves as hurt, betrayed or abused. Indeed, from the psychological and emotional point of view, I would argue that the pursuit and execution of justice is not an essential requirement in establishing lasting emotional comfort and allaying the unbearable emotional experience that follows from one person hurting another. They are two quite separate tasks.

I have already referred to the phenomenon whereby feelings that are pushed down will try, spring like, to push back up. There is a further simple emotional rule which states that feelings that are pushed down and left unexpressed remain inside of us in a kind of limbo state, neither expressed nor truly extinguished. This has been called emotional 'unfinished business' and is commonly experienced as a bodily pressure, something pushing uncomfortably outwards from within. It might take the form of a need to keep thinking or talking about the same things over and over, sudden bursts of feeling from out of the blue or a difficulty relaxing or being still for any length of time. In the simplest way, we might say that e-motion means simply to move outwards. Our emotions will forever try and do this. We are organically structured to respond emotionally to events and that response will follow a determined organic pathway. In addition to seeing and hearing and thinking about what happens, we also feel what happens.

It is perhaps helpful to think of our emotional reactions as having a beginning, middle and an end and we are able to interrupt this process at any time depending upon how we have come to feel about the relational consequences of having that particular emotion. For example, as a man I am adept at interrupting tearfulness, as was my father before me, and his father before him. In my family, the social price of expressing sorrow and tearfulness is (wrongly) imagined to be greater than the price of suppressing such feelings. Not unlike one of the characters in Wuthering Heights, Hindley Ernshaw[4], who's 'sorrow was of that kind that will not lament. He neither wept, nor prayed…' the men in my family are experts in interrupting the emotional impulse to sorrow and grief. They have carried themselves through life and relationship in fear of a humiliating outburst and consequently, of having to face the imagined relational consequences of this fear. Fear of abandonment, rejection or humiliation at times of greatest emotional need makes the suppression of grief essential. As for Hindley Kershaw, 'he cursed and defied; execrated God and man, and gave himself up to reckless dissipation.'

Being hurt and feeling wronged will commonly result in unfinished emotional business. Some feelings we have in response to being wronged are usually interrupted by being squashed or swallowed, spat out or displaced. This happens because we are unable to express such feelings, either because it is dangerous to express them or because our self-esteem cannot allow us to. As we have seen in the previous family scenario, this leads to a tragic, pernicious and corrosive inertia that has devastating effects on healthy life and relationships. My experience in 25 years of psychotherapy is of many, many clients presenting with unfinished business related to feeling wronged. An exclusive focus on the wrongdoer, and what they have done wrong, does little to help the deeper emotional needs. How they have been wronged, what has been done wrong, who has done wrong, the desire for exposure, the righting of the wrong, and seeking a social solution for this is one small part of the remedy. This book is about the other larger and, I believe, more crucially significant part of the remedy that involves paying attention to, and being able to bear, what it really feels like to be wronged and often to have to watch them get away with it.

CHAPTER TWO

It's easier to fall out of love than out of hate

As I wrote in the preceding chapter, my fictional family are not unique and psychological manoeuvres to comfort and self-soothe unbearable feelings has attraction, meaning and value for many of us. We commonly turn to blame and accusations, to violence and vendettas whenever we feel bad. This is particularly alarming given that a great many human beings feel bad a great deal of the time. We feel bad and unsurprisingly, and rightly, we search for what is wrong. All too commonly we then seek to identify who is wrong. From an emotional and psychological point of view it is this second step, of seeking the person of the wrongdoer and the act of wrongdoing, which is an unnecessary, potentially malignant and ultimately futile step.

Before moving on to further psychological exploration of this phenomenon, I would like to state a little more clearly what I mean when I say 'wrong', as there are different possibilities and each has its own distinctive associations and implications. When we say that 'someone's done something wrong' we are generally talking of something which is wrong in one of three ways. Someone might be wrong morally, ethically or instrumentally.

Moral wrongdoing will relate to a breach of a person's individual beliefs or values that are an essential part of the preferred identity of the person. If I act in an immoral way, I am doing something that runs counter to the personal values and the structure of what I have come to assert makes up 'myself'. For example, I might 'believe in' always telling the truth or that I should take care of my elderly parents when they get sick. Consequently, if I tell a lie or abandon my parents to the care of others then it could be said that I am, by my own principles, committing a moral wrong. However, it could not be said that I am absolutely or objectively wrong from all perspectives. In this sense, morals are essentially personal, idiosyncratic and generated from the emotional and psychological developmental imperatives of our own lives. The fact that they also may be widely shared or espoused as categorical and dispassionate does not diminish the personal underlying subjectivity of moral 'wrongness'. 'Moral reasoning' is an unsustainable and antithetical phrase which, to my mind, is based more on individual wishful thinking than verifiable proofs. For me, morals are a point of view and that view is constructed on the foundations of a combination of childhood anxieties and the processes of socialisation. Therefore, they cannot be said to be based on reason. To my mind, 'morality', and the value and imperatives it professes, is a highly personal construct based upon what makes a person uncomfortable or causes anxiety.

Early infancy is a chaotic and perplexing experience for any child and primitive psychological mechanisms operate to reduce the distress this might otherwise cause. In essence, such mechanisms work by splitting the world into 'good' things and 'bad' things and, through this mechanism, the infant makes sense, of and feels less anxious in, a capricious and unpredictable world. As the child matures and grows in intellectual power and emotional resilience they may learn to tolerate ambivalence and what was once black and white begins to take on shades of grey. This natural developmental process will be further directed and highly influenced by the pre-existing and prevailing moral (and ethical) values in the environment of the child. Thus, the roots of our morality lie in a combination of social conditioning and early psychological splitting processes. A mature moral stance may be more nuanced and complex but persisting at the core of the notion of morality are the twin emotional limitations of avoiding complex ambivalence and gaining social acceptance. For morality, that which we say is bad is that which makes us feel bad. This does not, of course, invalidate notions of morality or discount their worth as chaperones of all socialisation processes and guides to collaborative human behaviour. It simply allows the possibility that 'being wrong' in a purely moral sense is to be seen in the context of the person's individual life story and is not incontrovertible.

The common habit we have of asserting moral imperatives as universal 'truth' can create a potentially destructive social development because group moral posturing readily becomes moral tyranny. In terms of psychological and emotional needs it can be seen that declarations of moral wrongdoing are a vehicle for anxiety reduction. Inasmuch as our professed morality is both a product and a support of our emotional equilibrium then, insisting upon a shared and consensual morality is likewise a vehicle of social emotional and relational equilibrium. The degree to which this insistence is reinforced by aggression, or violence, reflects the degree to which the underlying anxieties are operational. Everyday phrases such as, 'we all think this is right/wrong' or, 'everyone should feel this way' should be subject to scrutiny when seen in the light of their anxiolytic function. It will also commonly be found that such statements frequently form the righteous core of any revenge scenario. The tyranny here is revealed in that it becomes highly perilous to openly disagree with the avowed moral posturing.

It has been said that morals are the way we treat people we know whereas, ethics are the way we treat people we don't know. Whilst morality can be seen to be constructed on a personal narrative it is useful to describe ethics as being built on the foundations of a systemic, or organisational, narrative. By this, I mean that ethical behaviour describes what is consensually right and proper within a particular social structure. Ethical values can be less subjective than morals and will primarily serve the needs of the social structure, rather than the emotional or psychological needs of the individual. Thus, the ethical is that which informs our behaviour in groups and in social and cultural encounters. Ethics is the foundation of the law and might rightly be claimed to be more considered, consensual and rationally based than morality. Although, here too I think it fair to point to a degree of emotionally driven 'rationality' in ethical deliberation and construction in that, the behaviour that is ethically 'wrong' substantially remains what disturbs us emotionally.

It is possible to see straight away that the moral and ethical might become intertwined. For example, a family will have both moral and ethical imperatives which may, or may not, operate in harmony.

The 'black sheep' of the family emerges from this kind of conflict. The recent cases of corporate and governmental whistle-blowers also highlights a conflict between moral and ethical values. Later in this chapter, I will look at marital separation and divorce in respect of the dynamics of claiming wrongdoing. The example of a divorce process also serves well as an illustration of conflicting beliefs in moral and ethical incompatibility creating an abundance of enduring hostility, misery and, of course, revenge drama. The divorcing couple may both claim immoral behaviour, unethical behaviour and illegal behaviour without being very clear as to which is which. It then becomes difficult to decide what kind of wrongdoing belongs where and where a remedy might be appropriately sought. What kind of wrongdoing belongs in the province of the solicitor, the judge, the friend, the therapist or the revenger? Each type of wrongdoing require different approaches and different remedies and it is the enduring misery of the divorce process that remedy and relief is commonly sought in the wrong place and from the wrong people. The moral and the ethical are commonly confused, and misused in the need to blame or vilify. Both equate wrongdoing with degrees of badness on a continuum from conflicting tastes, to mischief and naughtiness to malice, spite, cruelty and, occasionally, unlawfulness. To be unethical or immoral is not just to be wrong; it is be 'in the wrong'.

To be 'in the wrong' has personal inferences and relational implications that the third way of being wrong, the instrumental, does not. The instrumental might be described as that which is wrong because it doesn't work. If I display a lack of skill in a practical task, show ineptitude and naivety in human relationships through inexperience or lose at cards I am not 'in the wrong' in a way that might generate negative inferences about my moral or ethical standing. I am wrong simply because I have not learned to be, or do not have the skill to be, right. Unfortunately, it is uncommon for this kind of instrumental wrongdoing to remain unpolluted by a flavour of the moral or ethical. In our culture, where the denial of impotence and avoidance of humiliation remain a priority, any lack of skill or mastery in life is likely to bring emotional distress in its wake. It is not at all uncommon to be ridiculed or even hated for failing to do something that you simply cannot do. Instrumental failings can quickly become moral wrongdoings. The child who cannot, through no fault of their own, tie their shoelace or complete basic mathematics may become a target for ridicule and humiliation. Thus, they become 'in the wrong' in a way that goes beyond simple instrumental lack of skill or experience. However much we might tempted to translate the instrumental wrong into the moral or ethical, the reality of human limitation suggests that the purely instrumental remains. For this to be addressed with compassion, tolerance and understanding is as crucial to learning to tie a shoelace as it is to the growth of emotional maturity and the reduction of chronic human distress. Furthermore, if we return briefly to our family of the last chapter we might see that the situation becomes immediately more resolvable if we are able to shift the response away from moral and ethical wrongdoing towards a perception of instrumental wrongdoing. If we are able to see the psychological manoeuvrings and resultant behaviour of all involved as instrumental mistakes, and not as moral or ethical failings, a more fruitful and less injurious solution starts to become available.

In the story of our suffering family we will find plenty of opportunities for both moral and ethical judgements. With so much unhappiness and continuing heartbreak, hatefulness and misery, surely it has to be that someone is in the wrong? If we travel down this road there will be plenty of support for this view and many suggestions for possible remedies. Conversely, however valid the moral and ethical accusations may seem to be, they will only serve to maintain and prolong the essential underlying family drama of continuing schism, misery, hatred and revenge. I am proposing that, as an alternative, the family might find a way to abandon their desire to 'pay someone back' one day, effectively letting them get away with it, and instead address directly their hidden feelings of impotence, humiliation and loss. There is no moral or ethical judgement if we can say that this family is, from a psychological and emotional perspective, making an instrumental error by avoiding unbearable states of mind and feeling. If it becomes possible to approach the problems in this spirit, no-one needs to be 'in the wrong' and experience has shown me that a transformation of the chronic, inter-generational misery becomes more possible.

The instrumental 'wrong' is exactly the kind of wrong that is within the province of the psychotherapist. Psychotherapists make judgements about their clients, and the lives of their clients, all the time. They are both critical and judgemental and, hopefully, will share these observations with their clients. Whilst it might be difficult sometimes to differentiate between the moral and ethical and the instrumental, the psychotherapist has no business engaging in moral or ethical judgements regarding attitude or behaviour and interestingly, it would be unethical for them to do so. Such deviation from the psychotherapeutic task only serves to dilute the work and is an instrumental mistake on the part of the therapist. As I have tried to demonstrate in the case study, chapter 10, the key to effective and sustainable emotional resolution of experiences of wrongdoing lies in a painstaking psychotherapeutic process focussing on inner psychological impact and the consequences of harm. It is not to be found in a discussion of what someone else did or didn't do and how bad they might have been. Nor, is it to be found in emotional and psychological flights into denial or revenge.

If we are tying a shoelace, we know if it works or not and therefore can readily make criticisms, judgements and interventions based on principles of instrumental error. The question as to whether a human being is 'working' or not is not such a simple one and it is perhaps fair to observe that psychotherapists are often fairly opaque in describing their models of working, functional human beings. Even so, there is a model of health that has emerged from over 100 years of theory and practice and, like the medical model, does not require moral or ethical considerations to implement. Whilst psychotherapy[1] is not science, in the way that more falsifiable and verifiable disciplines might be, it has established a plausible authority on evolving working hypotheses of human psychic functioning, clinical practice and quantifiable outcomes. It is on this authority that the psychotherapist will base their observations, criticisms, judgments and interventions. In essence, this authority states that emotional and psychological development proceeds from an evolved organic process and, if appropriately supported by the environment, progresses through immaturity to maturity and thereby to healthy degrees of self-esteem and capacity for human relationships. If not supported, the development will arrest and result in various intra-psychic splits, defensiveness and anxiety states together with an incomplete repression of the general emotional and psychological personality. The repression, being incomplete, will manifest in one of many possible attitudinal, emotional, cognitive and somatic characteristic postures that will then obstruct healthy self-esteem and capacity for human relationships. In growing up in an imperfect world, we are forced to make compromises with our emotional health and such compromises come with a price. It is the psychotherapeutic task to examine both the compromise and the price and consider whether there might be possibilities for a more adaptive compromise, at a smaller price. One such compromise, arising from a characteristically unsatisfying childhood environment, and having a large price tag, is the revenge manoeuvre. Much has been written objecting to the revenge manoeuvre from the moral and ethical viewpoints and I will look at some of this helpful and constructive thinking later. However, of all our defensive manoeuvres it is perhaps also the one most in need of deep scrutiny from the standpoint of an instrumental error.

There is little doubt that in human relationships the revenge scenario has been around a long time. It is not new, appears to be a constant in our ways of dealing with each other and is a potent force in shaping our history. Having said this, I would also add that through my adult lifetime it appears to have become more prevalent and more visible in, to borrow Freud's phrase, 'the psychopathology of everyday life[2]'. I am using the term 'psychopathology' quite intentionally as I do think that this phenomenon can be understood as the product of a predictable but aberrant psychological state. My belief is that it is not human nature, or instinct, to seek and to take revenge but that it is a desire that emerges from a very particular facet of human consciousness and the impact this has on our emotional lives. My hope would be that in understanding this phenomenon we might go some way towards addressing the destructive presence of the revenge motif as it emerges for all of us in everyday life. In my work I have seen tenacious, and ultimately self-destructive, patterns of revenge playing out again and again in the everyday life and desires of many people. In 25 years of working as a psychotherapist, I have developed a view of revenge that I think goes some way to understanding why it is so ubiquitous and so relentlessly never-ending. In short, I have come to realise that the impulse towards revenge emerges from a need to protect ourselves from emotional and psychological pain. We seek and take revenge in order to defend ourselves from feelings of loss, impotence and humiliation and, quite simply, to re-find that lost state of mind and body where we can once more think well of ourselves. Whilst I am not making any claims to have found the answer to this riddle, I am going to present an interpretation that can be of use in situations where wrongdoing is being claimed, fairness or comfort is being sought and not found, and further harm ensues through the taking of revenge.

Take, for example, the instance of a person going through a divorce who can find no relief from the feeling that they have been terribly wronged and discovers that the law provides only partial remedy and relief. The person seeking redress in divorce is often dismayed to find that very few of the 'wrongs' that people engage in during marriage have meaningful remedies under the law. They are usually not illegal and whilst some may be taken into account by the law in terms of unreasonably coercive or controlling behaviour, they do need to be extremely unreasonable to have any impact in legal terms. Any legal remedy is therefore unlikely to be congruent with the degree to which the person feels aggrieved. In other words, what the law says is fair commonly does not feel fair. I have found this to be the case in many attempts at conflict resolution and is often why the attempt breaks down. Indeed, the chasm that exists between that which is legally, collaboratively (ethically) fair and that which feels fair is the rock upon which so many conflict mediation attempts founder and sink.

Confronted with the loss of a marriage it can often be difficult to discern which are the 'real' feelings and perhaps more to the matter in hand, which feelings should be attended to in order to find some comfort and relief. During divorce or separation, it is all too common for people to feel unbearably sad or angry, often vengeful, perhaps depressed and restless. They may be thinking and feeling the same things over and over again, sleeping badly and feeling physically ill. People can swing alarmingly between raging anger and helpless depression, feel powerless and stuck in a situation that seems to go on forever. The consistent emotional thread that emerges in disputed divorce situations is of being wronged and the belief that the other person is 'going to get away with it', together with an overwhelming desire not to allow this to happen. There is commonly a complete confusion and lack of discrimination between moral, ethical (sometimes legal) and instrumental wrongs as the person in their agony reverts to more primitive coping mechanisms. What was once grey is again black and white, what was once love is now hate and what was once mutuality of concern becomes vengeful and pitiless pursuit of the former partner. That this usually happens to both parties in the divorce, and both as a consequence feel threatened by the other, does nothing to help either of them step away from paranoid[3], aggressive and confrontational states of mind.

Parties to a divorce will expect that their lawyers will do their best in practical ways and within the legal framework, to find a solution to the conflict. However, divorcing couples will also discover that many grievances will not be addressed by the legal process and it is very common for them to be left feeling overwhelmed by painful emotions. This is especially true of the awful feelings of having been wronged and the consequences of this can be damaging to health, family, work and chances of future happiness.

What will most certainly not be addressed by the legal process are the terrible feelings of powerlessness, loss and humiliation. Feelings that are so difficult to bear and so easy to circumvent with rage. It is in such a situation that the emotional and psychological necessity to defend against this misery will easily erupt into revenge and hatred. In the maelstrom of chaos, powerlessness and humiliation that can be the emotional accompaniment to a divorce or separation, the certainty of righteous hatred and a desire for revenge can be seductively tempting as a psychological anchorage, a port in the emotional storm. The consequence is that divorced individuals can be still 'in hate' with their former spouses many years after the separation and to a degree that can poison all subsequent relationships. We saw this laced with tragic hideousness in the family at the beginning of this book and it does indeed seem far easier to fall out of love than to fall out of hate[4].

We might wonder why, when all the time and money has been spent, the court has said that this or that is fair, the mediation has said that this or that is fair, even the respective lawyers have said that this or that is fair and that 'fairness' has been signed, sealed and delivered, it so commonly still just doesn't feel fair. There continues to exist a world of difference between what is said to be fair and what feels fair. This reflects a dissonance between the subjectively constructed moral standpoint of the person involved, their particular psychological response to the emotional pain of feeling wronged, and the ethical standpoint of the institution of the law. It also demonstrates the presence of an instrumental error which, in the rush to blame and accuse, often gets completely disregarded by all – that no-one is in the wrong but still it went wrong and it feels wrong. In a painful and confrontational dispute there is often no place for ordinary human frailty when every disappointment and loss become a moral or ethical wrongdoing.

I'll stay with the example of the divorcing couple as it is so familiar to many people but also allow that the principles unfolding are applicable to many situations where someone feels wronged by someone else. I have been told, on two occasions by different solicitors, that a divorce judge will think they have got it about right if their judgement feels equally unfair to both parties. This may sound frivolous but does illuminate something of the unavoidable consequence of any conflict resolution that does not pay adequate attention and sensitivity to the subjective emotional experience of what feels fair. A 'feeling' of fairness is not simply the result of a mediation of objective and verifiable measures but will also be vague and mutable, capricious, often contradictory and deeply personal. It will be formed and tempered by individual tastes, values and prejudices and built upon the experience of a profoundly unique life story. Given this, it is perhaps easier to understand the truthfulness in the judge's statement and we might be justified in saying that just because something doesn't feel fair it doesn't necessarily mean it isn't – and vice versa.

Many people involved in a divorce dispute will claim that they just want a fair deal and to move on with their lives. As mentioned, there are two distinct aspects to this idea of 'fairness'. One is the equity that the law will propose that is likely to be rigid, impersonal to a degree and based on the historical, ethical consensus of the whole community. Secondly, the individual and subjective feeling of fairness that is likely to be fluid, personal and based upon a singular and unique moral perspective. From these two perspectives it is easy to see that a conflicted outcome is imminent and the divorce process will either stall badly or one or both of the people involved will be left with deep emotional grievances following the settlement. Each and every wrong becomes a moral wrong as it is appropriated by the personal rage and indignation of both people in the dispute. This appropriation serves to build an impenetrable bastion against ambivalence and reality that might otherwise reveal ordinary human shortcomings. In such a way we might avoid irresolvable feelings of loss, failure and disappointment at the way life has turned out. It is almost impossible for accusing anger to co-exist with disappointment and heartbreak; the one usefully cancels the other. This is indeed what happens frequently in divorce proceedings and it is very difficult to negotiate a way through this without an understanding of the very powerful emotional and psychological processes at work. I have heard divorce lawyers despair at the unreasonableness, the bloody-mindedness, the stubbornness and the vengefulness of their own clients. Sometimes this erupts, inappropriately and wrongly placed, and the dispute overflows to become a dispute between lawyer and client. As the emotional maelstrom bucks and tips, the sense that someone's doing something wrong is very readily transferred from one person to the other – biting the hand that feeds, or is just trying to help. The client who sacks their lawyer because they 'just don't get what I mean by fair' or won't agree to do what I want (and get what I want), will be transferring the revenge impulse temporarily from the spouse to the lawyer. This easy transferability of the object of our revenge, from one person to another, is a significant clue in helping us see that revenge has little to do with external, ethical justice and fairness but is more about finding internal, emotional and psychological comfort. As long as we feel that we have paid someone (anyone) back we might feel better. For the frustrated lawyer it might be helpful to consider, however difficult it is in the passion of the moment, that the person is being unreasonable, bloody-minded, or stubborn and revengeful for good reason. That is, if they weren't being unreasonable, bloody-minded, or stubborn and revengeful they might well be being shattered, humiliated and utterly bereft. The revengeful person is desperately attempting to push away some wholly unbearable feelings that would otherwise overwhelm them.

We could ask the question: why are some feelings more unbearable than others? Why might we choose to feel outrage rather than say, grief or feelings of powerlessness? Why might a person set out, often at great personal cost, on a seemingly endless pursuit of 'justice' that is fuelled by hatred, vengeance and an absolute inability to let them get away with it? I think the answer to this lies in the ability of the revenge scenario to offer an assurance of redemption, which stems from the central illusion and irresistible promise that if we can make them feel the way we feel, we will not feel it anymore and furthermore, will be master of those feelings. The successful prosecution of revenge holds out the tantalising promise of a transformation of the individual's internal condition from an unendurable state of impotence, humiliation and grief to one of dominion, self-pride and self-possession. It is a magic wand of unimaginable value. The promise and illusion of mastery over unendurable feelings, dominion of others and, above all, control over hurt and humiliation is the seductive promise offered by the revenge scenario. In fantasies of revenge, the promise of relief from inner torment is truly irresistible.

There is no doubt that to be swamped by hurt and powerlessness in the wake of insult and then seized by an unexpressed impulse to revenge, can be a deeply unpleasant experience. Prior to action, the person who seeks revenge will be held in a profound spasm of physical contraction and in the grip of an excruciating state of anxiety, combined with an overwhelmingly energetic and restless, ill-defined impulse to 'do something'. An acute need to resolve and relieve this highly uncomfortable state of affairs will consume the revenger's conscious awareness to the exclusion of all else. As these tremendous forces coalesce into a thought, they will come to rest on one central idea and desire – that of not letting them get away with it by paying them back. The awfulness of this condition cannot be overstated particularly, as is commonly found, they have already got away with it and, in truth, there's nothing the revenger can do other than take revenge. Who would not wish to be master of this deeply unpleasant state of affairs and what better way than to pass it on to someone else and, if they've done something wrong and unfair, don't they deserve it?

I have already suggested that other emotional responses to being wronged, such as powerlessness or depression, might be less palatable given our need to think well of ourselves. The promise of mastery over the self and others is not readily sustainable in the face of feelings like grief, helplessness and humiliation. From a psychological perspective, it is entirely possible to avoid such feelings and there is a whole raft of defensive manoeuvres available to reduce our subjective state of relative vulnerability and anxiety. Such manoeuvres are generally learnt by trial and error over the period of our early childhood on the principle that what seems to work in the particular circumstances, sticks. The preferences we build over these early years will depend upon our innate characteristics and dispensations together with the support our chosen emotional strategy might get from those around us. We will also take on emotional characteristics by copying what we see others doing and what seems to work for them. Occasionally we may learn to do the opposite of what we see around us but even this remains a strategy dictated by a particular family environment. Taken together, the constellation we come to depend upon and take, mostly unthinkingly, into adulthood forms the characteristic way that we look after ourselves from an emotional perspective. Psychotherapeutic theory teaches that there are several characteristic and commonly employed defence manoeuvres. They all rely on some form of splitting of awareness, or self-knowledge, which then results in a distortion of perception. It is the distortion of perception that enables us to feel better when we feel bad. Those of us who have grown up in environments where distortion of reality is necessary for emotional survival, for example frightening or abusive environments, will have developed such manoeuvres far into adulthood and they will be a fixed feature of personality.

Psychological defence manoeuvres[5] are alike in being a way of not knowing what we might otherwise know. They can be very helpful both emotionally and cognitively as it can be comforting to see things other than as they are. For example, if I am unloved it might be preferable to conclude that I am to blame rather than that the person whom I wish to love me simply cannot, or will not, love me. In this way I comfort myself by imagining that if I am to blame then perhaps I can do something about it. The alternative is that I am not to blame and therefore powerless to do something. Self-blame can bring illusions of power. It is important to emphasise that defensive manoeuvres are not 'bad' things in themselves; they are the ways in which we have learned to look after ourselves. However, because they involve a distortion of reality, and a slightly different distortion for each one of us, they will make human relationships, communication and understanding more convoluted although, some might say, also more intriguing and creative. In brief, the distortions might be categorised thus:

Denial – a simple refusal to acknowledge that which is probably true, either consciously or unconsciously. 'I am not angry with you' might mean I am not angry with you or, that I am angry but afraid to show it or, that I am angry but don't know that I am angry.

Repression – pushing out of consciousness what is probably true away and is a kind of amnesia. 'I do not remember anything before I was 12 years old' might be a form of repression, a forgetting motivated by an emotional need not to remember.

Regression – returning to an earlier state of emotional functioning, usually motivated by stress of some kind. Often, feelings of vulnerability or anxiety that are generally overcome may be temporarily overwhelming again, as they were in childhood. 'I feel like a two year old again because my wife has left me'.

Displacement – an example might be that we arrive home and kick the cat or shout at the children because we cannot express our frustration and anger at work as it might be more dangerous to do so.

Projection – a manoeuvre that results in someone else having attributes or feelings which, in truth, belong to you. Projection is the basic manoeuvre of scapegoating and prejudice. It involves taking a personal characteristic, of which we are afraid or disapprove, and imagining the other person carries that characteristic. For example, if I disapprove of my tendency to criticism and judgement of people I might develop a persona of acceptance and toleration but imagine that the world around me is very critical and judgemental.

Reaction formation – expressing the very opposite, and hostility towards, what is probably true about your own desires. Primarily motivated by envy and in our culture many feelings related to avarice are very commonly dealt with in this way. For example, 'he's such a show off, always with a new girlfriend on his arm...unchristian behaviour, I'm sure he'll come to no good'.

Intellectualisation – talking 'about' feelings instead of feeling them, in effect staying out of your body and living in your head. For example, 'yes, of course I can get excited; I just don't see the point'.

Rationalisations – explaining feelings as if they are nothing to do with you, or as if they were rational responses, through fear of showing emotion. For example, replacing 'I' with 'one' or 'you' when talking about personal experience is a common example.

Sublimation – sometimes seen as a healthy defensive manoeuvre in that it refers to the transformation of unbearable emotional states into productive activity thereby providing an illusion of possible mastery. 'I became a policeman after my sister was attacked'.

The revenge scenario, as we shall see in detail in the next chapter, is highly sophisticated in that it makes use of all of these manoeuvres and thereby explains its enormous appeal as an effective psychological defence. It is possible to review the forgoing list and see that the revenge scenario manages to embrace elements of all. Indeed, I would call revenge the 'defence of all defences' in that once activated and fully operational in all its psychological and emotional mechanisms, it effectively makes all other individual defences redundant.

Revenge might be codified as in the case of the vendetta, or feud, and in this form has been repeatedly portrayed in history, in art and literature. It is immediately recognisable for what it is. That the story of insult, dishonour, revenge and restitution is so often revealed as a tragedy goes some way to uncovering the absurdity of this highly addictive human behaviour. It is not my intention here to debate whether or not revenge is a good or bad thing, if it is ethically justifiable or even if it is indeed a reasonable and appropriate response to hurt. This is for the ethical philosophers, moralists, theologians and politicians to propose and debate. My interest in this book, as a psychotherapist, is to understand the construction and execution of the revenge scenario from the point of view of psychological and emotional necessity. From this perspective, the revenge scenario and its attendant psychological and emotional manoeuvres, is instrumentally wrong. It does not work as a reliable, sustainable and enduring balm and comfort to the hurt it seeks to remedy. For this, we need to look much deeper into ourselves and seek a strategy that proves to be less violent and corrosive; more successful, sustainable and instrumental.

CHAPTER THREE

A man that studieth revenge keeps his own wounds green

The phenomenon of revenge might be seen as amongst the most enduring and significant features of human relationship throughout history. At its most complex, varied and tenacious it is found in all human societies. It manifests in some guise of the psychological manoeuvre described in the previous chapters – that someone's done something wrong. A wish to pay someone back for what they have done wrong will add intention, clarity of thought, planning and drama and provide energy, stability and focus that incoherent rage or righteous unfocused anger alone cannot do. I have already said that this may not be so much to do with real, external wrongdoing and the desire for justice but more about a need to soothe aspects of the self in the face of unbearable feelings. What I am going to suggest and explore for the rest of the book is that to concentrate on what someone has done wrong, and to pursue revenge, is more to do with trying to feel good about ourselves, to think well of ourselves, than with any externally defined ethic or desire for justice, retribution, deterrence or punishment. In other words, revenge is aimed at putting something right inside ourselves rather than putting something right out in the world.

I have previously described revenge as an irrational act because it is motivated by emotional necessity rather than cognitively formulated needs and desires. The emotional and psychological drivers to revenge have nothing to do with ethics, although they may assume the guise of a very personal and apparently righteous morality. The psychological cascade that is the revenge scenario commonly follows an identifiable trajectory that might be described thus: the cascade begins with a very personal injury that insinuates an awareness of vulnerability to hurt. It then proceeds quickly towards an idea and the strong conviction that someone's done something wrong. Next to emerge is the feeling of personal insult, of 'being wronged', which in turn leads to anger and righteousness and finally a wish to make the wrongdoer suffer, because we have suffered. Relief is obtained by making the wrongdoer feel the way we feel, instead of us. The creation of a revenge scenario is virtually instantaneous in some people and the cascade, once begun, is almost unstoppable. It bears repeating that the cascade has little to do with justice and is formulated primarily to protect ourselves from psychological and emotional distress. In essence, it is an attempt to protect us from three things: powerlessness, humiliation and grief. It is an attempt to do something about these three emotional states; how unbearable they are and to make them go away from consciousness, without actually feeling them.

This way of discharging the power of a difficult or frightening emotion, without actually feeling it, is the nature and purpose of all emotional defence mechanisms. The psychological cascade that is the revenge manoeuvre is possibly the most favoured of all complex human emotional defences. This may go some way to understanding why it is at once the most ubiquitous of human experiences, an enduring literary and artistic theme and the source of an endlessly seductive, yet ultimately illusory, appeal. The central intention and characteristic of the vengeful act is that it contains the intention to pay someone back. It is the attempt, often taken at some personal cost or risk, to impose suffering on those who have made us suffer, because they have made us suffer. This is motivated not by a desire for justice but because the person seeking revenge can imagine no other way to redeem the personal feelings of powerlessness, humiliation and grief that have accompanied the original insult. In taking revenge we are, in fact, seeking to pay back those feelings, often in the guise of executing justice, which we cannot bear. We are seeking to transfer the unendurable feelings from ourselves to the identified wrongdoer and in this we find relief.

It seems important at this stage to try and define in more detail what I mean by the 'revenge scenario'. How might I define revenge if it is to be separated from ideas of justice, punishment and from other ways of putting things right in the world that someone has made wrong? Might it be, as many have said, a human instinct or a part of human nature to think, feel and behave in this way? Should we understand it as a social phenomenon or perhaps as a peculiar fluctuating manifestation of the human psychological state? The evidence of history, also perhaps of common sense and personal experience, would probably lead us to believe that revenge is indeed an inseparable part of what it is to be human. Can a propensity for revenge be viewed as something instinctual or an evolved survival mechanism, an eye for an eye? If so, this might go some way to explaining our extraordinary success as a species of animal. To pursue, attack and destroy those who have done us harm does appear, on the face of it, to be a good strategy for continued individual and group survival.

As human beings appear to be the only animal to engage in the revenge drama, this may go some way to explain our pre-eminence and dominion in the natural world. However, if we look deeper into the complexities of our psychological and dynamic emotional lives, we discover elements of the revenge response that might lead us to other interpretations. Furthermore, the discovery of alternative interpretations may have the additional advantage of opening the possibilities of finding different, less destructive and more adaptive responses to those who do us harm. It is clear that in terms of a response to those who do us harm, revenge serves to increase the totality of harm and violence that human beings wreak amongst themselves. My view is that revenge is not human nature. It is not a genetic predisposition nor is it inevitable in human relationships. Therefore, we are presented with the possibility of behaving differently. To do this however, we need to appreciate the actual dynamic psychological, emotional and social function of revenge and to carefully consider the implications offered by this understanding.

When I was a child at school we would play a game called 'tig' or 'tag' or simply, 'it'. The game was very straightforward in that the child who was 'it' would have to chase and touch another child who then became 'it', and so on. The game could go on forever. The pleasure of the game was in chasing, and being chased, in avoiding the touch and in taunting whoever might be 'it' at that moment. It was enormous fun to chase and be chased, to touch and be touched, to taunt and be taunted. In a less charming extension of the game, a special favourite of the boys, a child might become 'it' by virtue of having done something seen to be repellent by the rest of the group. Any potentially humiliating behaviour would do, like, for example, accidentally stepping in dog mess, or something similarly delightful to little boys. The game thereby took on another dimension and the imperative to touch someone else, and thereby pass on the humiliation, became far more urgent and vital. The flavour of the game changed as excitement became tainted with anxiety and the taunting became barely masked cruelty involving potential humiliation. The personal significance and pleasure that might otherwise be conferred by being 'it', the centre of the game for a while, became a double-edged sword in that the price of significance was now, potentially, a humiliating torment. Happy days.

One of the tortuous difficulties of this game, and particularly when it had progressed to the second variant, was the impossibility of extinguishing the humiliation. It could only be passed on, the game could have no end and someone must be left with the discomfort of still being 'it'. The solution to this would be found in a form of group collusion that enabled the group of friends to return to unity and fidelity. The child who was 'it' at the end of the playtime would be able to re-join the group, and get rid of their humiliation, if they could collude in choosing an outsider to pass it on to. It might be that this chosen outsider would be unaware of the game and, even better, if they could be someone of superior status, a teacher for example. The touch could then be carried out surreptitiously, fully witnessed by the group, and the humiliation passed on without the danger of retaliation as the new 'it' was unaware that they were now 'it'. In this way, the former 'it' could pass on their humiliation and even gain a degree of pride through the approbation of their friends for their audacity and cunning. This tactic sees the victim enlisting the help of his potential tormentors in identifying an outsider. It is acceptable in that it keeps the group cohesive and is based upon a shared awareness and empathy for the agony of whoever might otherwise be left carrying the humiliation within the group.

I think it is possible to see, even in this relatively benign children's game, the beginnings of a more troublesome social predicament. If we were to translate this to an adult drama it is possible to see the ease with which the different and wrong 'it', the scapegoat, arises from the need of a group to think well of itself and to maintain cordiality, unity and mastery of unpleasant feelings. For the purposes of thinking about a new definition of revenge, the game can also serve to reveal many of the characteristics of the scenario. This can be helpful in beginning to define some of the relevant and distinctive features of the revenge scenario:

- The presence of someone who is 'wrong' in some way, which puts them at a disadvantage in respect of the 'rightness' of the rest of the group.
- In addition, the 'wrongness' carries a meaning that is felt as humiliating or status-diminishing to the person.
- An aggressive anxiety to pass on the 'wrongness' to another.
- An equally aggressive anxiety of the rest of the group not to be in receipt of the 'wrongness'.
- A pleasure in the group being 'right' or, probably more importantly, 'not wrong'.
- The temptation to turn this game into something that involves an outlet for primitive aggression and possibly envy, sadism and violence.
- The temptation to turn this game into something that serves the needs of the group for identity and cohesion in being 'not wrong' or 'not like them out there'.

Once again, to re-cap and summarise some of the features, we can see that the revenge scenario is an irrational manoeuvre in that it is driven first and foremost by emotional necessity, not by rationality, and exists in order to protect us from anxieties related to otherwise unbearable feelings. The revenger wishes to make the other person experience suffering as they have and to hear the unbearable feelings instead of themselves. Like the childhood game, it is a zero-sum game in that the suffering cannot be extinguished, only passed on. The terrible anxiety of retaliation persists. In this kind of game we can temporarily end our individual suffering but we cannot end the game nor can we end the inevitable anxieties such a game produces.

I have attempted to show in the following chapters that, because we carry an evolved consciousness of the self in relation to others and to ourselves, and because the game of 'it' might be seen as relationally atavistic, relational anxiety can be seen to be at the root of what it is to be human. Ironically, it is largely because of the enduring presence of anxiety in our lives that we characteristically commit many instrumental errors in the way we try to relieve this anxiety. The anxious human seeks, first and foremost, to reduce their anxiety and this leads to many instrumental errors in behaviour and emotional processing. We seek only to reduce anxiety and not to resolve the 'game'. To turn against each other in an attempt to pass anxiety on does nothing to reduce the totality of anxiety, nor does it eliminate anxieties relating to retaliation. My view is that many instrumental errors stem from thoughts and behaviours that focus solely on immediate relief from anxiety. We might otherwise explore more emotionally challenging, longer term, sustainable solutions that attempt to 'solve the game' and reduce the totality of anxiety. It is the central intention of the revenger to reduce their anxiety, not to look at how and why they are so vulnerable in the first place. Revenge commonly employees overkill to prevent retaliation, trying to eliminate future anxiety. It does nothing to encourage harmonious and anxiety free relationships but revenge has attraction because of its simplicity and its economic capacity to use current grievances and load them up with past insults. It is characteristic of the revenger to use a present situation of wrongdoing as a vehicle to settle old scores even if historical grievances are far removed in terms of the people or timescale involved.

In respect of the natural world our species, Homo sapiens, appears to be the only animal to engage in revengeful practices and this may well be because of the peculiar feature of human consciousness which we call 'consciousness of the self.' As we shall see more fully in Chapter 5, consciousness of the self, combined with sophisticated intelligence, generates a penetrating sensation of individual value and significance that extends beyond organic significance and appears to be unique to our species. Alone in nature, we carry the double-edged sword of a peculiar human consciousness that leads us to believe we signify value and consequence as individuals, over and above our organic relevance. However, self-significance, when faced with a capricious and unpredictable world, creates anxiety by rendering injury to the same a real and ever on-going possibility. It is from such injuries that the impulse to revenge arises.

Revenge can be seen as a type of retaliation, like for like, although not all retaliation needs to be revenge. Retaliation might be strategic, rationally thought through and aimed at a specific outcome in the world. For example, the threat or actual carrying out of aggression and injury against a threat is deterrence, not revenge. The essential character of retaliation that is revenge lies in seeking satisfaction and inner relief from psychological torment that appears to follow on from paying someone back. The revengeful element may well include a well thought out plan and be premeditated, but it will always embrace the notion that the subject has been 'made to pay' for their wrongdoing. The flavour of the payback will typically be vindictive, sadistic and malicious and result in a subjective reduction of anxiety and increase in pleasure for the revenger. They are 'made to pay' by being forced to endure the feelings that previously resided in the revenger. The retaliation that is revenge demands the fierce evacuation of a bad feeling from one person and the pitiless insertion of that same bad feeling into another person.

Acts of revenge are therefore a particular kind of retaliation but it does not always follow that any actual offence or wrongdoing has happened. Just as there is no necessary correlation between reality and desire, there is equally none between one person feeling injured or offended and any wrongdoing having taken place. It is entirely possible, and unfortunately very common, for illegitimate grievances to give rise to revenge. For example, revenge might be sought and taken for humiliations that are not offences, such as unfavourable critical observations, the turning down of a job application or the failing of a driving test. It is enough for the revenger to feel injured, and to translate this into a sense that someone has done something wrong, to initiate the psychological cascade and set them off seeking revenge. Furthermore, experience shows that where the original source of injury is unavailable, or forgotten, a substitute will do just as well. That the focus of responsibility, the 'who' of someone's done something wrong, can be transferred readily onto a proxy further supports my view that the primary motive force in revenge is not external justice but internal psychological and emotional equilibrium.

Therefore, we can say that revenge can occur where no real offence has been committed; it is only necessary that the revenger feels wronged. Thoughts and acts of revenge can be, and often are, misdirected, indirect or indiscriminate. However, successful revenge will always involve paying someone back in such a way that the psychological and emotional torment of the revenger is believed to have been transferred from the revenger to the revengee.

We can further isolate revenge from other forms of response to hurt by differentiating their accompanying emotional states. In other words, they can be identified by examining the different psychological and emotional constellations and manoeuvres employed in each case to achieve some degree of satisfaction or comfort. I will return to a more detailed exploration of these distinguishing features in Chapter 9 so perhaps it is enough at this point to note the superficial differences. A desire for justice emanates from moral and ethical indignation, born of cultural norms and constructions of wrongdoing. These norms and constructions in turn are based upon a largely rational ethical consensus with regard to injustice, meanness, wickedness and other misconduct, including that which is formalised in the law of the land. Revenge, on the other hand, is born of massive anxiety about the need to re-establish the self-image, particularly related to humiliation and power, and employs all the resources of our most psychologically primitive self-protective mechanisms that are essentially schismatic and violent in nature.

As a justification for action, revenge has been the subject of ethical contention and a great deal of individual moral ambivalence. Typically, and especially amongst the thinking elite and ethical scholars, it assumes the negative attributions of unseemly motivation where it is often considered immature and primitive. Socrates[1] advised restraint in the face of injury and counselled that greater satisfaction would be obtained by keeping the temper. Aristotle[2] held that a virtuous person will bear accusations and slights with moderation and will not rush hastily to revenge. Likewise, Francis Bacon[3] in 1597 wrote, 'a man that studieth revenge keeps his own wounds green which would otherwise do well and heal'.

I have already suggested that revenge is an irrational act inasmuch as it is motivated by emotional imperatives. This appears particularly so if we are to consider alternative rational, outcome-oriented, forward-looking ethical deliberation. In the light of rationality, the backward orientated nature of revenge is incompatible with social progress and the contemporary need to demonstrate the ascendancy of civilised and rational human behaviour over the primitive. It would be attractive to imagine that rational and civilised peoples (and by implication, mature and cultured peoples) protect their interests but also, let bygones be bygones and cut their losses, learn their lessons and re-build lives. The revenger, on the other hand, typically refuses to forget a wrongdoing and will focus their attention on undoing what has been done and what, as a consequence needs to be done. The revenge scenario is backward looking and driven solely by emotional imperatives although this may well be disguised by an overlay of rational protestation in the guise of a call for justice and human rights. In the grip of a revenge scenario it appears almost impossible for contemporary persons to behave in any way other than what we might have preferred to consign to our primitive past.

In addition to the rationalist argument against revenge, I think it is fair to say that revenge, in contemporary ethics, is widely regarded as improper. This position of disapproval would be reinforced by those virtue theorists and religious ethicists who emphasise the ethical importance of our motivations. In other words, as purity of motive must be taken into account in the consideration of the ethical value of any action, revenge would be viewed as ethically impure. Likewise, further objections would arise from any ethical position that puts its emphasis on the strategic importance of motivation and action and its translation into social norms, laws and policies. For example, from this point of view, to pursue revenge could be seen as a strategic error. We have seen in Chapter 2 that the strategic error of pursuing revenge as part of a divorce process might lead to a terrible and painful stalemate. The law does not support what it would view as an emotionally motivated strategic error. This is yet another form of rationalist objection in that, for example, to seek satisfaction from revenge can lead to frustration, thereby compounding the resentment and impotence that the revenger was intending to relieve. Further, the pursuit of revenge often becomes self-destructive in that revengers lose perspective, become consumed by hatred and inflict disproportionate, or indiscriminate, harm. Revenge commonly escalates into endless cycles of revenge and counter-revenge involving vendettas and the development of culturally constructed codes of injurious behaviour. Where vendetta develops the essential quality of the revenge is lost as the behaviour evolves into a duty in the absence of any personal connection to original wrongdoing. Such collective acts of revenge are thereby considered by the rationalist to be primitive in nature and part of a less well developed social ethic.

However, the rationalist viewpoint is based on the premise that human beings are indeed rational beings and are able to construct social and personal relationships along rational lines. This seems to me to be wishful thinking in the face of evidence. It appears to propose that the rational human being will ascend and develop by virtue of cognitive rigidity and by exercising acts of well-intentioned will over the vicissitudes and powerful imperatives of our emotional selves. My view is that to propose that we are essentially rationally motivated is another instrumental error in that it wilfully ignores and underestimates the irresistible irrational influences of anxiety and desire in the human condition.

However, the most common objection to revenge comes from what might be termed the 'respect for the person' ethic. In essence, this position argues that revenge is always morally indefensible in that it derives satisfaction from the intentionally accomplished suffering of another person for no purpose other than the sake of the suffering itself. In her admirable book, 'Forgiveness and Revenge', Trudy Govier[4], takes this position and transposes onto it notions of forgiveness. The book is a good example of an objection to revenge from an ethical standpoint and, with respect to the author, it is worth employing her thesis for a moment as a contrasting backdrop so that we might deepen our understanding of the non-rational and non-ethical objections that I will be proposing. In my view, the notion of forgiveness as a response to injury is redundant and, at worst, somewhat grandiose. However, Govier's opinion is stated from the outset of the book:

> 'that seeking revenge is objectionable for both practical and moral reasons; that the desire for revenge is not deeply natural in the sense of being an elemental, culturally independent feature of human nature; and that even if revenge were to be natural in that way, such naturalness would not constitute a moral argument in its favour'

I can agree with her proposition that revenge is not natural. She also seems to me to be entirely correct when she writes elsewhere in the book that the remedy for the desire for revenge lies in 'a process of overcoming attitudes of resentment and anger that may persist when one has been injured by wrongdoing'. Where I would take issue is in her definition of 'attitudes' in that these are far more than just cognitive phenomena. I would say that the attitudes (of resentment and anger) she refers to are manifestations of emotional processes that have their roots in deeply entrenched, resistant, and commonly unconscious, psychological mechanisms. If we are to seek to change 'attitudes' it can only be through careful and painstaking attention to these underlying dynamics otherwise the change will be superficial and based solely on a fragile act of will. Acts of will are all well and good until confronted by a degree of stress and anxiety that usually results in fragile emotional imperatives re-emerging and dictating behaviour in ways which we may find ethically regrettable but emotionally expedient. I would agree that cognitive phenomena alone may well be able to be transformed by ideas of forgiveness but the revenge scenario is cognitive only in its planning and execution. In its origins, development and motive power, it is entirely irrational and hence, immune to rational and ethical modification.

100 years of psychoanalytic and psychotherapeutic theory and practice have demonstrated that the power of conscious and unconsciously embodied, highly resilient and irrational psychological mechanisms will not be overcome simply by ethical imperatives, acts of will or well-meaning fortitude. When the rationalist 'respect for the person' thinkers cite the ethical and consequential failings of acts of revenge they are being ingenious yet ultimately circular and undermined by the evidence of thousands of years of ordinary human behaviour and the absolute ubiquity of, and a marked preference for, the revenge scenario. Their desire to lead humanity to a higher ground is to be applauded and yet their project falls down in their reliance on reasoned ethical, often theological, argument alone. They point repeatedly to revenge as primitive, irrational and a failure of the 'higher' values that we might aspire to. In describing processes of 'forgiveness' or in proposing rational, instrumental arguments as an alternative to revenge they are advocating what is little more than an act of will based upon a desire to be a superior kind of human being.

Whatever we may think of acts of revenge from an intellectual and ethical standpoint, the fact remains that in general people do not invariably consider malicious, envious or spiteful revenge shameful, distasteful or even morally wrong. In many people, myself included, there remains a moral ambivalence even to the most extreme acts of revenge. As I have already mentioned, morality emerges from highly personal experience and is constructed on the ground of an individual narrative of meaning and personal significance. As a consequence, personal morality is not rational, nor culturally cross-consensual and there is no evidence to support a conformity in moral repugnance to revenge. For example, when an ordinary person commits an act of cruel and sadistic violence they may feel an amount of remorse and guilt and will often receive the censure of society. However, when a large enough group of ordinary people commit the same act, they commonly feel a sense of pride and will often receive the approbation of society.

Shared difficulties in tolerating feelings of powerlessness, humiliation and loss do appear to lead to a wide forbearance of violently revengeful behaviour in the quest for relief from such feelings. Whilst there is some degree of squeamishness and wilful ignorance at the amount of violence or overt sadism that may reveal itself, revenge remains a socially acceptable and generally encouraged response to those who do us harm. I do not believe that philosophical, ethical or theological appeals to behave differently and become ethically superior kinds of human being will ever bring significant and widespread change to social behaviour in this respect. For this to come about, even in limited form, I think we need to dig a little deeper.

CHAPTER FOUR

The sweetest kind of drunkenness

Can we really be justified in condemning those who engage in revengeful practices as unrefined primitives and those who disdain revenge and practice forgiveness or forward-looking rationality as ethically superior? Is this the best we can come up with as an objection and remedy to this most appalling, devastating, viscous, hateful and enduring of human behaviours? I fear that if this is indeed the best we can do, then little about revenge as a habitual and socially sanctioned human behaviour will change.

Contemporary ethical theorists tend to relegate instrumental and revengeful violence to the iniquities of primitive cultures. A quick look at the history of contemporary civilisation will show us that this is far from true. Modern man's widespread and socially sanctioned practice of revenge is, at its core, an intentional act of violence carried out with all the precision required to inflict at least as much harm, and commonly much more, as was inflicted on the revenger. That the act of revenge always involves a considerable degree of intentional violence in order to carry it off is central to all ethical objections. Rational objections are less vociferous on this point as violence continually proves itself to be highly efficient at achieving its stated goals. The rational objection also founders here as it comes to rely on the less rational premise that rational men are also, by implication, civilised men. A degree of non-rational squeamishness seems to have percolated the rationalist position. Rationalists and ethicists make claims that the progress of theology, of humanism and the development of civilisation have made violent reactions redundant or, at least, disagreeably regrettable when the civilised person has no other recourse. Regrettable or otherwise, history teaches us that human beings are not at all averse to considerable acts of violence. In the absence of temperance through ethical considerations such as empathy and compassion, or more prosaic concern about threats of punishment or retaliation, acts of violence are generally regarded as the most expedient and easily accessible means of establishing and maintaining both material and psychological security. This is as true for contemporary civilised man as it is for unrefined primitives and I see little evidence to support propositions of human progress towards a different ethic.

I want to be as clear as possible about what I mean by violence. In particular, to distinguish the aggression at which the human being is so adept from the kind of aggression that the greater part of the rest of the natural world engages in. Violence is a human phenomenon and can be distinguished from natural aggression, which can also result in physical and emotional harm. Aggression is to be found elsewhere in nature although is mostly either impersonal or instrumental and functional. Violence, in contrast, is relational and inter-personal in that its carries a meaning beyond that of the functional. In my terms, the aim of violence is to establish or maintain a hierarchical relationship in respect of individual significance that goes beyond the needs of organic survival. Violence is intended to create dominion over and above that required for physical survival. Thus, violent acts are defined by their personal and relational meaning above and beyond the immediacy of the moment and the degree of violence will reflect the strength with which the aggressor wishes to impress their meaning. Planned violence or elements of cruelty, sadism and excessive harm are employed to the degree that is felt necessary to get the relational meaning across and in a way that will be remembered. Violence intends to convey a message of relational superiority by humbling the recipient.

Violence is rarely purely instrumental and wholly impersonal and might be properly identified by one or all of the following characteristics: firstly, violent acts committed with the intention of doing personal physical harm, inflicting physical discomfort, pain or death upon a person. Secondly, violent acts are those that make postures and threats to inflict personal physical harm in a similar way. Thirdly, violent acts inflict harm, or threaten to inflict harm, on persons or possessions upon whom an individual relies for feelings of emotional or material security and safety. Fourthly, violent acts are intended to cause fear through threats or actual acts involving loss, abandonment or separation from significant persons or possessions. Finally, violent acts are those that are intended to injure the person's self-esteem through emotional cruelty, ridicule, shaming and humiliation and intentional exposure to others. If we can accept this definition of violence, and a differentiation from organic functional aggression, then it is not difficult to propose that violence is one of most pervasive and effective means of socialisation employed by human beings throughout history and the most expedient method of attaining hierarchical ascendency. The satirical cartoonist, Ralph Steadman put it boldly when he said recently: 'Authority is the mask of violence' (Steadman, 2016)

Aggression, of itself, need not be violence. If I am engaged in hunting for meat or in protecting myself from predators, I may well resort to a considerable degree of aggression and inflict significant harm, even death, on other living beings. If I am witnessing my child being threatened or harmed in some way I would most likely, in the immediacy of the moment, employ any amount of force necessary to remove the threat. Again, this may well result in injury or death but I don't think it would be reasonable in any of these instances to speak of my actions in terms of intentional and cognitively motivated intent to inflict personal hurt and distress. Such aggression is impersonal and functional. My motive is essentially reactive and I am using protective aggression. It is essentially 'for' my child, rather than 'against' the potential threat. Of course, we could well imagine, in the second example, the use of force becoming more than is necessary to remove the immediacy of the threat. The necessary aggression might now be called violence but, this will also depend on an analysis of the motivational and relational intent involved in the aggressive acts. We might justify the use of excess force in terms of removing the immediate and any future threat but, possibilities exist with instrumental and functional aggression for it to extend into what might be called 'comfort' violence, which is the revenge scenario. 'Comfort' violence is violence that is surplus to the requirements of physical protection and is exacted in the service of generating or redeeming self-esteem and relational domination.

The notion of 'excess' or 'surplus' aggression is a well-established feature in psychotherapeutic theory and it would be useful to review it in order to attempt to be clearer about how we might distinguish between aggression that is necessary and appropriate and that which is violence. This is far from easy as one person's 'necessary and appropriate' will be another person's abusive violation.

The psychotherapeutic theory of neurosis[1] is essentially that family, or societal, restrictions on the free expression and full autonomy of infants and children result in a contraction of the organic vitality and the emotional processing capacity of those children. The neurotic symptom results from the conflicting demands of cultural imperatives and individual, organic autonomy. Neurotic structuring is the attempt to make a compromise between free organic expression, the desires and demands of the child, and the authority of socialisation. Over 100 years ago, Sigmund Freud highlighted this phenomenon as a causative agent in the production of various neuroses but also viewed such repression as necessary for social life to operate. He recognised that this social compromise would lead to inevitable neurosis but viewed this as the necessary price of civilisation. Furthermore, he stressed the necessity of the authoritarian social structure as a buffer against primitive barbarism. Freud believed in the fundamental primitive barbarism of human beings and his discovery and exposition of this essential civilising compromise remains one of the cornerstones of the psychotherapeutic endeavour to this day.

Somewhat in support of Freud's view, modern social theory[2] has likewise emerged through the twentieth century as a means of trying to understand human behaviour and, in particular, the dynamics of social organisation. However, in contrast to Freud's emphasis on internal psychological conflicts and interaction with prevailing culture, social theory has been more concerned with the fragmentation of the self, and neurotic structuring, which results from authoritarian structures and hierarchical social relationships. Specifically, social theorists have focussed on the prevailing systems of power in society and the ways they impact on an individual's psychological and emotional life. In short, Freud was more concerned with how the inner life of the person meets the outer life of culture and social value whereas social theory identified the impact of social culture and value on an individual's psychological life. Integrative endeavours, psychoanalysis meeting social theory, have produced attractive and highly persuasive theories seeking to explain the plight and subsequent behaviours of modern human beings. Having some relevance to our enquiry is the work that emerged in the second half of the twentieth century from what became known as the Frankfurt School[3].

The Frankfurt School was an informal association of largely Marxist-orientated academics who were affiliated with the Institute for Social Research, founded in 1923. The focus of the Frankfurt school was an attempt to establish a comprehensive and compelling critique of the points of interconnection between culture, society and the human psyche. Some of its most celebrated thinkers were the psychoanalyst, Erich Fromm[4], the philosopher, Herbert Marcuse[5] and the sociologist, Theodore Adorno[6]. Following on from Wilhelm Reich[7], a one-time protégé of Freud, they sought to explore an amalgam of the social, political and psychological dynamics of the dissatisfaction, fragmentation and alienation of human beings in the modern world. They were seeking a unified theory that might explain why human beings appeared to be incapable of organising a society within which the mass of people could live healthily and well, without unnecessary conflict, violence, poverty and anxiety.

A fine and honourable intention and for the purposes of this enquiry I want to highlight one relevant concept that emerged from this group of thinkers – that of 'surplus repression'. According to Herbert Marcuse, domination of the child's free expression and desires (repression, as described by Freud) kick-starts a chain reaction that leads to no less than an enslavement, which is the hallmark of modern civilisation. Furthermore, this chain reaction is circular inasmuch as the enslavement leads to rebellion, which in turn leads to more domination. This domination is, in his view, everywhere underpinned by a threat and actual use of forms of violence. The relevance here to the theory of neurosis is that the dominated person, fearful as they are of the violence that will descend if they do not submit, will firstly submit and secondly, ingest and metabolise the repressive commands and injunctions into their own psychological make-up. That is to say, they swallow the repressive imperatives and make them their own. The neurotic symptom results from the struggle within the person, consciously or otherwise, to reconcile organic vitality, freedom and potency with the strictures and reproaches of a hierarchical and repressive socialisation. Both Marcuse and Adorno proposed that this kind of psychological repression underpins all forms of social organisation and that the 'reality principle' is formally structured (and thus unavoidable) through ideological, political and economic forces.

The 'reality principle' was Freud's original conception of the authority of the Father; the necessary force to which the child must submit in order to become a functioning member of civilised society. As did Freud, Marcuse, Adorno and Fromm also accepted that an amount of basic repression is necessary for the functioning of society. However, they argued that this repression need not be absolute, nor even so much as is generally supposed by an anxious establishment that is fearful of the autonomy and power of their children. Their objection is to 'surplus repression', meaning the element of repression that is generated in the service of authoritarian political and economic organisation. More specifically, the element of repression that is over and above the minimum required for society to operate in a co-operative, consensual and safe way. According to this view, surplus repression functions to serve political and economic inequality. In effect, it deepens the basic, necessary repressions in the interest of domination within authoritarian social structures. According to Marcuse, the chief features of this domination are: restrictions on sexuality as a result of the ascendancy of the patriarchal-monogamic family and a division of labour based on inequalities of individual worth and the atomising influence of an overly commodified culture. In a direct echo of their inheritance from Wilhelm Reich, Marcuse boldly states: 'the desexualisation of the organism is required by its social utilisation as an instrument of labour[8]'.

The ideas contained in the concept of 'surplus repression' can lead us back to being able to define violence as surplus aggression. In other words, forms of aggression that exceed the needs of organic survival but exist in order to serve the requirements of a particular artificial and culturally created authoritarian or hierarchical social arrangement. Surplus aggression is violence and is a central legitimising and organising agent in our social arrangements. In all authoritarian social structures, the violent act stands always fully prepared to arise in support of that structure. This appears to me to be the case whether this is the structure of the family or the nation state. The fact that we are so adept at transforming surplus, violent, aggression into what is called 'necessary and appropriate' does nothing to change the nature of the thing but does reveal how much we have ingested, and made our own, the authoritarian and inequitable social, political and economic systems that rely on it.

For examples of surplus aggression dressed up as necessary and appropriate to survival we do not need to look far. It is one of the towering achievements of modern, and not so modern, humans that they are able to turn one into the other with such easy mendacity and sleight of hand. Human beings are very fond of waging war on each other and generally manage to translate violence that is executed in the service of hierarchical emotional and material security into necessary and regrettable aggression. History is replete with examples of massive societal collusion in these deceptions and reflects how much individual psychological and emotional imperatives might be translated and extrapolated into national and global strivings.

When a nation embarks on a violent crusade to fight tyranny, to promote peace and freedom, or to counter a perceived threat, it is reflecting the same psychological dynamic as when a school teacher humiliates a child into submission or a parent hits a child for being naughty. The justifications are the same and yet we must suspect this as simple, violent, expediency in the service of domination and the imposition of questionable hierarchical and political values. Once begun, the prosecution of international or civil war is mostly supported by the general population and this mysterious collusion might be understood if we can see that the warmongers are doing on a national scale what is nonchalantly done on a daily basis between individuals, in families and in small social groups. The path to war is usually dressed in a coat of many splendid colours and yet on closer examination it looks very much like the cascade to revenge I described at the beginning of the previous chapter: the perception of harm done or the threat of harm leading to an awareness of vulnerability, leading to massive anxiety, leading to the belief that someone's done something wrong, leading to identifying and violently paying back those who have wronged us. In this light, we might also add that revenge, and the process of revenge, can be pre-emptive and a response to an insult to esteem that has not yet happened but we fear might happen.

I do not wish to make an anti-war case here but simply to highlight that, given the underlying psychological and emotional dynamics that lead to war it is, like revenge itself, instrumentally wrong, futile and will inevitably generate more of the same. The prosecution of war and even victory in war will do nothing to address and change the deep psychological vulnerabilities that lie neglected at the heart of the original impulse to violent action.

Given the reality of what actually happens when people go to war, at first glance it may be puzzling why warfare is so much a regular and generally acceptable part of ordinary life. My view is that warfare is so familiar, enticing and acceptable simply because the underlying personal and emotional dynamics are so personally familiar, enticing and acceptable. The following few paragraphs are examples of familiar, enticing and acceptable warmongering and the use of staggering degrees of surplus aggression. Each one, with a few minor dissenting voices, was successfully initiated and executed through manipulation of human vulnerabilities in the face of fear and with the empty but seductive promise of relief from anxiety and redemption of personal and national esteem. Revenge and pre-emptive revenge dynamics by and large shape human history.

That most gentlemanly of southern gentlemen, Robert E Lee, was the son of General Henry Lee, a friend of George Washington and a representative of one of the wealthiest and most respected families in Virginia. Born in January, 1807, he grew up with all the advantages wealth and family position could give in a Republican land. He received the best education afforded by the institutions of his native state. On the eve of the Battle of Gettysburg, Lee was married with seven children and a confirmed member of the Episcopal Church. A much civilised man. He was also the commander of the Army of Northern Virginia and, in the summer of 1863, chose to invade the northern states. The campaign culminated in a battle that began on the first day of July of that year. Over the next 3 days, the battle would end the life of some 51,112 men and boys in some of the most brutal circumstances imaginable.

In Gallup's list of widely admired people of the 20th century, John F Kennedy came in third, behind Martin Luther King, Jr. and Mother Teresa. Catholic, a self-professed peace loving family man, John F Kennedy famously said: 'Pay any price, bear any burden, meet any hardship, support any friend…to assure the survival and success of liberty.[9]' In the early stages of the Vietnam war, Kennedy allegedly agreed that America should finance an increase in the size of the South Vietnamese Army and that an extra 1000 US military advisors should be sent to South Vietnam to help train the South Vietnamese Army. Both of these decisions were not made public as they broke the agreements made at the 1954 Geneva Agreement. Later, Richard Nixon, who by 1969 had taken over the reins, was quoted as saying 'Let us understand: North Vietnam cannot defeat or humiliate the United States. Only Americans can do that[10]'. By the time of the American defeat, humiliation and withdrawal in 1975 an estimated 3.4 million people had lost their lives as a result of the war. In 1986, the American journalist, Martha Gellhorn[11] suggested the actual, and continuing, reason for disquiet about this 20 year-long act of anti-communist hubris.

'America has made no reparation to the Vietnamese, nothing. We are the richest people in the world and they are among the poorest. We savaged them, though they had never hurt us, and we cannot find it in our hearts, our honour, to give them help - because the government of Vietnam is Communist. And perhaps because they won.[12]'

Horrifying, though perhaps not surprising to note, that 10 years after the end of the conflict the revenge scenario, fuelled by humiliation, was still operative and that even the bewildering body count was not enough to satisfy it. Another well documented example concerns the ex-British Prime minister and 'pretty straight sort of guy', Tony Blair. He spoke of his decision to invade Iraq in 2003 saying, on a well-known ITV chat show and alongside a popular American actor, 'I think if you have faith about these things, you realise that judgment is made by other people ... and if you believe in God, it's made by God as well[13]'. 13 years on from the invasion of Iraq, clearly a further act of civilised man in pursuit of civilisation (and of God's will, it seems), it is estimated that between 120,000 and 140,000 non-combatant civilians have lost their lives.

The World Health Organisation has calculated that in the early years of this millennium for each year, a little over 1.6 million people died as a result of intentional violent acts carried out by other human beings. The report astonishingly, though perhaps wishfully, concludes that 'violence is neither an intractable social problem nor an inevitable part of the human condition'. A quick search of the internet reveals that 180 million people died violently as a result of armed conflict during the twentieth century. To put this in perspective, the population of the United Kingdom currently stands at a little over 64 million. As I write there are currently 11 major armed conflicts in the world resulting in more than 1,000 deaths per year and 34 armed conflicts resulting in fewer than 1,000 deaths per year. I cannot find any evidence to show that any of the protagonists, on either side, claim the death and suffering to be anything other than necessary and appropriate. It seems that, apart from prosecuting violence on a massive scale, we are also highly adept at attaching acts of violence to established, positive, cultural values thereby making it possible to claim such acts as civilised, legitimate and entirely justified. Just like revenge is felt to be.

The figures quoted above pale into insignificance when we start to consider the greatest form of violence that humans are capable of. It is called the unequal distribution of resources and is a political choice we have made. As with acts of warfare, the violence that unequal distribution of resources inescapably produces is justified by acts of political and intellectual deceit and creative sublimation to sidestep culpability. Global poverty, whilst not carrying the 'regrettable, but necessary' flavour of intentional direct violence that is warfare, remains an appalling form of violence. However, like warfare it too is commonly described as 'regrettable', 'unavoidable' and, worst of all, a natural fact of life on this planet. We are at the beginning of the 21st century and approximately 25,000 people die every day of hunger or hunger-related causes, directly attributable to poverty. This is one person every three and a half seconds.

Through repetitive acts of creative sophistry, civilised people have been able to maintain the illusion of moral superiority, of human progress out of a primitive barbarism, whilst simultaneously indulging a taste for domination through extreme violence. Sigmund Freud wrote in 1930:

> . . . men are not gentle creatures, who want to be loved, who at the most can defend themselves if they are attacked; they are, on the contrary, creatures among whose instinctual endowments is to be reckoned a powerful share of aggressiveness. As a result, their neighbour is for them not only a potential helper or sexual

object, but also someone who tempts them to satisfy their aggressiveness on him, to exploit his capacity for work without compensation, to use him sexually without his consent, to seize his possessions, to humiliate him, to cause him pain, to torture and to kill him. Homo homini lupus (man is wolf to man)[14].

That human beings are capable, and all too ready, to engage in prolonged and excessive violence is beyond question. The questions that arise as a consequence, and are of import to this book, relate to the provenance of this violence and how it is that our particular species has evolved, seemingly alone, with such a pronounced capacity and insatiable appetite for it. To be clear, I am referring to violence as excess aggression in the sense that it exceeds the needs of organic survival, for hunting or protection from predators. Furthermore, an excess aggression in which the conscious intention is to inflict harm in order to reduce anxiety, to gain emotional comfort and relational material and social advantage.

We might turn to the archaeologists and evolutionary psychologists for an explanation. However, surprisingly, there is very little evidence for innate or instinctual excess aggression and a propensity for violence in our species. Indeed the widespread and popular belief in innate human excess aggression, whilst popular in contemporary storytelling, is not supported by archaeological evidence. The earliest recognisable humans were not violent killers and evidence suggests that for at least 4 million years, they lived in small groups rearing their young and maintaining material security without excess aggression and probably in co-operation with other discrete groups. The earliest identifiably human-like animals emerged around 4.5 million years ago in the central and east/southern parts of Africa and they lived in wooded areas and were principally vegetarian. By 3.5 million years ago they had vanished and were superseded by an upright-walking tree-climbing 'southern ape' (Australopithecus) who became known, after the Beatles song, as 'Lucy[15]'. Lucy is succeeded by another Australopithecus (africanus) around 2.5 million years ago who in turn made way for the first of the Homo lineage: Homo habilis, who had brains 1.5 times larger than the Australopithecines. Homo habilis are found butchering animals with simple hand tools but there is no evidence that they were butchering each other.

Homo erectus emerged around 1.8 million years ago and appeared simultaneously in east Africa, China and Java. Gradually,

Homo erectus spread to populate the Near East and Eastern and South-East Asia and by 500,000 years ago the diaspora had reached the European continent. Simple and more sophisticated hand tools, notably symmetrical pear-shaped stone tools, are ubiquitous amongst these early humans and are found in all parts of the world. For the next 35,000 years the diaspora continues and tool making becomes more and more sophisticated until some 150,000 years ago Homo neanderthalensis (Neanderthal man) arrived. This was followed by the emergence, around 80,000 years ago, of the first of our own species, Homo sapiens. 40,000 years later artistic artefacts and personal adornments began to appear, along with cave paintings. Up to this point, recognisably human ancestors have been around for 4.5 million years and for 2.5 million years of that time have possessed a large brain comparable in size to modern humans. Yet, there is still no archaeological evidence that might indicate excess aggression or violence within the species. These people appeared to live alongside each other and reserve their aggressive propensity for what is necessary for hunting and to protect themselves against natural predators.

It is only in the past 20,000 years, as numbers of Homo sapiens' begin to rapidly increase, that evidence shows wandering groups coming into competition with each other for food and space. Conflict over resources, and probably sex, erupted and set the scene for what we see to this day. The archaeological record of violent aggression within our own species - as demonstrated, for example, by stone projectiles embedded in human bones - dates only from this period, and no earlier. This is more than 100,000 years after humans became morphologically modern and about 30,000 years after the emergence of art, grammatical language and complex social relationships. It appears that somewhere along this path, spanning a mere 20,000 years, humans decided that the advantages of violent competitiveness outweighed those of a non-violent co-operative, co-existence. This is too short a timescale to be explained as an evolutionary change and can only have been a behavioural one, founded on cognitive and emotionally informed choices. Excess aggression and extreme violence towards one another is indeed a startling feature of modern human history but as there is little or no evidence of it in pre-history, a proposition of a genetic or inherent propensity in the species is not supportable.

A more convincing proposition is to consider increasing proximity of human beings, the resulting competition for limited resources and the developing conscious awareness of self-importance in relation to the social group. As human beings became more numerous, they competed not only for material security and physical domination but also for relational ascendency, emotional security and the elimination of anxiety. The increasing perception that 'there's not enough for everyone' following these limitations would generate a natural survival anxiety in any animal. It might be assumed that this competitive imperative led to anxious human beings finding, for the first time in the natural world, a novel and devastating use for their astounding cognitive and creative potential. Highly explosive when combined with a genetic inheritance of a highly complex intelligence and natural animal aggression.

Relative to the rest of the animal kingdom, humans have very large and sophisticated brains, including areas of specialised intelligence that can work across different behavioural domains. The human brain is a very powerful, flexible and functional tool when geared to the task of surviving and thriving in an overcrowded and potentially hostile environment. Humans learn by trial and error, by observation and imitation and by generalisation from specifics. The use of violence, being largely effective, would be reinforced by experience and result in the modern humans we are today. Homo sapiens are animals of devastating biological effectiveness, exceptionally ruthlessly intelligent and absolutely adapted to survival, where necessary, through violent domination, exploitation and extermination.

As I mentioned earlier in this chapter, violent acts can be defined and differentiated from organic aggression by their personal and relational meaning above and beyond the immediacy of the moment. A violent act is both a demonstration of a capacity for aggression and a statement of relational potency. By taking the act of aggression above and beyond that required for immediate organic survival we are transported into the realms of relative self-significance and self-esteem. As I have already described, revenge has a zero-sum potential and this stems partly from the common belief amongst people that self-esteem is likewise a zero-sum phenomenon. It is generally believed that self-esteem can only exist in relation to other self-esteem in a way that is proportional, one to the other. We measure our esteem against that of others and it is very difficult to conceive of equality in this respect. Like in the childhood game of 'it', we imagine that esteem can only be taken from others, or be taken from us, and is heavily dependent upon an illusion of social gradation. Such a belief may be a throwback to atavistic anxieties about the impossible co-existence of two alpha-male or females in any social group but, more likely, it is a product of an underlying vulnerability and anxiety that has been learned through the socialisation processes of an authoritarian and hierarchical culture. Thus, in the person seeking not only organic survival but also individual narrative significance that very significance, and its concomitant self-esteem, becomes a scarce resource and something our anxieties lead us to believe we will have to compete for. This reveals a further level of understanding of the function of excess aggression in that not only might it serve the needs of the macro-authoritarian social, political and economic structure it will also come to serve the more micro-personal necessity for relative self-significance.

Cultural imperatives of self-significance and self-esteem generally support potency and domination over those people who are seen to be of lesser significance or esteem. They are relational in their definition of value. Violence and excess aggression is commonly employed to establish and maintain such a domination. For the anxious animal that we are, the successful execution of excess aggression is a potent vehicle for appropriating mastery, security, admiration and self-esteem. Furthermore, it can be the means of redemption for the otherwise humbled, the impotent, the insecure and the brutally self-critical. For many such individuals the ecstatic opportunity to transform self-hatred into self-pride, hell into heaven, through an act of revenge is irresistible.

Psychological and emotional necessities towards revenge reach their most complex and dangerous form when we see individuals and groups engaging in a joyous obsession with apocalyptic violence which is, at its heart, nothing more than a desire to pay back, like for like, the hateful and abusive world that has so injured them. Consider this:

> 'This land was never one to reward virtue, but it was always strong in taking revenge and punishing evil. Revenge is the greatest

delight and glory. Is it possible that the human heart can find peace and pleasure only in returning evil for evil? Revenge is an overpowering and consuming fire. It flares up and burns away every other thought and emotion. It alone remains, over and above everything else…vengeance…was the glow in our eyes, the flame in our cheeks, the pounding in our temples, the word that had turned to stone on our throats on our hearing that our blood had been shed…vengeance is not hatred, but the wildest, sweetest kind of drunkenness, both for those who must wreak vengeance and for those who wish to be avenged[16]'

This description comes from a 1958 autobiography of youth, by Milovan Đilas[17], who emerged through the partisan movement of the Second World War to be a leading Yugoslav Communist politician, theorist and author. His book is a startlingly moving and fervently written account firstly, of his childhood and family and secondly, of the political, racial and religious feuding that shaped his part of the world. In modest, yet highly engaging prose, Milovan Đilas describes the leadership responsibilities of the family he was born into and the influence of the debts of blood that permeated the community. In the passage quoted, he is describing the emotional and violently passionate nature of such feuding which, in addition to the dread and horror he describes elsewhere, gives an intense portrayal of the magnetic core of the revenge scenario.

Thus, the first step onto the bridge from the ethical to the psychological and emotional might be served by looking at the cultural practice of the codified vendetta or the blood feud. In such instances the 'righting of wrongs' and justice are one and the same thing and intimately entwined with the idea of revenge; an eye for an eye. The vendetta is driven by responses to insult and is also carefully regulated by social norms and rules of behaviour that allow for revenge. The codification and regulation of revenge recognises not only material harm but, crucially, injuries to personal esteem and honour. Reparation must be such that not only material loss is restored but also that honour is re-established. Following a complaint and scrutiny of the insult or loss, the elders of a community will dictate and oversee the appropriate avenging injury, which in addition to material reparation can and often will include murder of family members. The blood feud occurred with regularity in pre-modern societies for example, in Iceland, in the Balkans and in other Mediterranean countries and in

Indian tribes on the American continent. Central to all blood feuds is the notion of honour, which permeates the idea of self-esteem in feuding societies, and it is this that generates and sustains the ethical norms of revengeful behaviour. Here is a good example of where, contrary to our culture, personal morality is likely to be in close conformity with ethical norms. In such societies 'honour' is the attribute of free, independent, potent men and is achieved through domination and the exercise of power over those who, by virtue of this, become less free, less independent and less potent. Honour is achieved by humiliating (in the literal sense of the word) others or those who previously had honour. The process relies on taking honour from those who are seen to have it. No honour is gained, for example, by dominion over women, children or servants. Honour conveys personal advantage by being attached to notions of scarce personal worth and esteem. The man of honour has material, positional and sexual advantages over the dishonoured man and significantly, for our purposes, he thinks well of himself. His image of himself is one of potency, pride and both material and non-material wealth. Furthermore, this image is one that he might well commit considerable acts of violence to achieve and maintain.

One advantage of this formalisation of the revenge scenario is that it may well serve to contain and limit its otherwise infinite capacity for destruction. In the absence of culturally imposed rules, limits and boundaries on what is an appropriate and proportionate act of revenge, the cycle of revenge and counter-revenge may well progress to the destruction of whole communities. However, the system of codified and structured honour and esteem does appear to pose the same difficulty we saw earlier with the childish game of 'tag'. That for someone to be honourable, someone else has to be dishonoured. This inevitably leaves the community in a constant state of anxiety; the roles can be reversed at any future time. The 'honoured' of today can so easily become the dishonoured of tomorrow. Again, as we have seen earlier, this is likely to generate a barrier to otherwise truly intimate relationships founded on trust, fidelity and truthfulness. This said, the experience described earlier by Milovan Đilas clearly describes a state of heightened vigour, dynamism and joy arising from the pursuit of revenge.

Herein lies the first clue in approaching a deeper understanding of the psychological and emotional function of the revenge scenario:

that carrying out successful acts of revenge can bring joy, meaning and heightened self-worth to the revenger. Such an act has the potential to transform a person's inner emotional attitude from an unendurable state of impotence, humiliation and grief towards a state of dominion, self-pride, self-possession and a feeling of mastery of themselves and others and of their anxiety-laden environment.

CHAPTER FIVE

The greatest invention in the history of life

I am hopeful it is now becoming clear that the forces underlying the impulse to revenge belong to the part of the person that is concerned with establishing and protecting a pleasing self-image. Along with its emotional components of anger, self-righteousness, hatred, sadism and envy, various forms of relational violence are generated in response to injury. Such violence is always in the service of re-establishing the revenger's good feelings about themselves. In this respect, the good feelings will be particularly related to feelings of potency, self-respect and honour amongst peers. It can be quite difficult to define what is meant by self-esteem as it has many names and is often obscured by cliché and jargon: self-regard, ego, pride, honour, self-confidence, self-belief, self-reliance, sense of self and self-assurance are all ways of describing our feeling about ourselves. This is then qualified by being good or bad in some way. In essence, self-esteem is a general emotional state reflecting the sum total of a person's inner judgements about their own worthiness. Another way of defining self-esteem is that it is a combination of self-confidence (a judgement of relative potency) and self-respect (a judgement of relative personal worth) and the resulting emotional state will always be rooted in a sensory experience.

Feeling good, or otherwise, about yourself is first and foremost just that, a feeling, a sensation and only secondarily, a thought. This fact arises from the developmental processes in early infancy where the awareness of ourselves as a unique and separate being proceeds from sensation and not from cognition. Differentiation between 'me' and 'not me' first appears in consciousness via three kinds of sensation: proprioceptive (the feeling of my body in space and in motion, relative to itself), exteroception (the feeling of the outside world) and interoception (the feeling of my internal state, hunger and pain are examples). It is true that the intellect and, eventually, language will increasingly mediate between these disparate sensations as a coherent image of the self as part of, but separate from, the world emerges. The cognitive image will coalesce from disparate sensory perceptions garnered from life events and will be the framework upon which self-regard will eventually be built.

The developing infant will gradually translate sensory experience into a representation of what kind of person he or she is and will make a relationship with that representation. In very simple terms, he or she will gradually come to feel pleased or not pleased with themselves. Self-esteem is therefore essentially a subjective phenomenon in that it is constructed from our own personal conclusions and attempts at formulating meaning and value. While such conclusions can be wildly at odds with reality they will be consistent with the sensory and emotional perceptions, meanings and needs of the child. For example, if mother doesn't love the child, a small child will very likely eventually conclude that this is because they are bad and unlovable. This stems from the organic reality that the child needs to feel loved (for the child love equates to safety and absence of pain) and therefore if they do not, something is wrong. As the child makes sense of the world essentially in a relational way this may quickly and tragically become: 'someone is wrong'. The child depends upon their mother to meet all their needs so, to conclude that she is bad would be far more distressing and frightening than concluding that they themselves are bad. The self-regarding relationship (or otherwise) builds gradually from such deductions until eventually the child has constructed an image of itself and formed an emotional relationship with that image. The child will simultaneously build a sensory experience of themselves, impose cognitive meaning and value and develop qualitative feelings about this aspect of themselves. The relationship that the child established with its sensory and imaginary self will form the basis of self-esteem, for better or for worse. The foundation of self-esteem is sensory but as the child grows it becomes increasingly complex as literal and figurative thought intervenes, language and relationships arbitrate and encounters with the self-esteem of others modifies, enhances or corrodes it. However, it still remains that core selfhood is constructed on a core of sensation and not thought.

It is therefore important to recognise that in adulthood we are motivated primarily by the quest for particular emotional states and, only secondarily, cognitive states. When I say to someone, 'I feel good today' I am describing a sensation, which I might then explain or justify in thinking or language. The essence of the experience I am communicating is embodied in one, two or all three of the sensory modes: proprioception, exteroception and interoception. It is precisely in this way that the elusive concept of self-esteem might be identified. It is defined primarily by sensation and only translated and understood through thought and language. It follows from this that self-esteem is not dependent upon the validation of morality or ethics and we do not need to be good in order to feel good. The quest to think well of ourselves is not dependent on good deeds but upon embodied sensation. If we can learn anything from witnessing a full-blown revenge drama, we will see that it is possible to engage in the most appalling acts of cruelty and violent brutality, think very well of ourselves and experience immensely pleasurable sensations. As with the saint or the philanthropist, the serial killer is likewise driven by the quest to think well of themselves.

The two very earliest challenges of life are to establish a sense of separateness, to become an individual and identifiable person, and to achieve mastery of pleasurable and non-pleasurable sensation. Being in charge of the feeling about ourselves becomes of vital importance once the process of differentiation into a 'self' has begun. It is at these early stages of life and in negotiating such difficulties that we learn our first lessons about power, control and mastery. Mastery of feelings about ourselves (both sensory and imaginary) form the core of potency in early life and how we achieve this will set a pattern of behaviours and beliefs that persist into adulthood. I will write much more about the importance of these patterns in later chapters although it is relevant here to highlight one aspect regarding such mastery. In very simplified terms, we can achieve good feelings either by turning to ourselves or by turning to others and, in practice, most people do a combination of both. However, the relative degree to which we might depend on turning to others will likewise dictate the degree to which we are dependent on how the other person thinks, feels and acts. If we learn early in life that we can only feel good when other people do exactly what we need them to do, we will need to develop strategies for controlling and changing people into the very things we need. At its most extreme, this dependency will manifest in controlling, manipulative or overtly violent behaviour as we attempt to force the people around us to behave in ways that support our good feelings. This is exactly what the revenger is doing when they, by taking revenge, are trying to manipulate and control events and people. The revenger is desperately dependent on others for their good self-esteem and this is why it is so difficult, impossible even, for the revenger to imagine letting them get away with it. If they get away with it, they are actually getting away with the revenger's good self-esteem. The desperation and violence inherent in the revenge scenario stem from a belief that reclaiming self-esteem cannot be done in any other way. The revenger has no faith in an independent source of self-esteem. It can only be had by taking it from others. In later chapters, I will return to this theme many times but enough here to begin to see the connection between relative degrees of dependency on others and a dependency on taking revenge. The correlation is exceptionally strong and established at a very early stage of life during first encounters with struggles for mastery over a pleasing, personal, sensory equilibrium.

In practice, the two tasks of becoming a person and achieving mastery of good feeling are one and the same thing. It is sensation that propels us to become aware of a separate self and simultaneously, mastery of this very same sensation (pleasure seeking, pain avoidant) is an anxious necessity. Pleasure seeking/pain avoidant imperatives remain of central importance throughout infancy and childhood socialisation processes so that all compromise, however complex it may appear to have become, will be rooted in such experience. For example, as a child I may find myself faced with a choice between an authentic, organic expression of hunger and a fear of abandonment or punishment. Perhaps, a choice must be made between expression of anger and a fear of retaliation or, (the schoolboy's nightmare) a need to urinate during school time and a fear of ridicule. In each case there is simple frustration of an organic need but also, through the relationship involved, possibilities of painful emotional states arising related to power and humiliation. If fear of the 'bad' relational consequences dominates organic need then we are able to maintain the 'good' relationship. We do not get abandoned, there is no retaliation and we are not ridiculed. The price, on the other hand, is that we have to find mechanisms for overpowering our organic needs. This is most commonly achieved by physical contractions of the body which, over time, become chronically disabling in so many ways. We may also be left feeling that our dignity has been injured; we have been overpowered, have been 'made' to choose you over me, and are perhaps shamed by our weakness, dependency and cowardice. Often, the child will find that they are choosing the least bad feeling and this may involve abandoning their own organic needs, swallowing the shame and feigning nonchalance.

Sometimes we do something bad to ourselves because of the fear of someone doing something worse. In the simplest terms this is the genesis of the neurotic compromise and the beginning of the struggles we have in establishing and maintaining good feelings about ourselves. For example, we may fail in some pursuit and then tell ourselves we didn't really want to win anyway. Such a compromise can help us cope both with the failure itself and the social humiliation of having been seen to have failed. A neurotic compromise is the understanding we come to with ourselves in order to reconcile the feelings of self-betrayal and self-abandonment with the need to be safe, socially acceptable and cared for. These understandings, the deals we make with ourselves become an integral, though generally corrosive, part of our self-esteem. Such mechanisms are one of the keys to understanding the function of revenge in that such self-insults, abandonments and betrayals, humiliations and accusations of cowardice might readily be redeemed by paying someone back later.

Self-esteem, good or poor, is the sum of emotions we have in relation to ourselves. In the same way that we think and feel about other people, self-esteem is the totality of all the things we think and feel about ourselves. We might ask: what is it like to be me? What it is like to be living with me right now, to be living in my body, with my relative sense of mastery of living, with my personality and accomplishments, with my relationships with other people. Am I pleased with myself? Truthful answers to some very simple questions will give each of us a sense of our own self-esteem and the relative security of our hold on it. We might begin to ask ourselves questions about the stability and security of our self-esteem; how vulnerable is it to being injured, how does it get injured, do I have characteristic ways of protecting my self-esteem from injury. Again, truthful answers to these questions will give us some indication of how much our self-esteem depends on other people's behaviour. How much do we feel our self-esteem belongs to us, rather than something that has been given to us by others and therefore, can be taken away? Important questions because a simple rule of thumb is that the degree to which we feel our good self-esteem does not belong to us, is not our possession and can easily be taken from us by other people, will be the same degree to which we may resort to revengeful thought and action when we are hurt or insulted.

In the natural world the modern human is the only animal to engage in revengeful practice and it also appears that they are the only animal to be conscious of possessing a self-esteem that exceeds organic survival needs. I think the two things are intimately connected. Both these phenomena can be viewed as things that separate humans from other animals and it can also be shown that self-esteem itself springs from a very particular facet of human consciousness. The 'particular facet' I mentioned in chapter 2 becomes relevant again here and I want to write more about it, specifically its development as a distinctive human characteristic. I am referring to the capacity of human beings to simultaneously create feelings of consciousness and ownership of that consciousness. Whilst the mechanics of consciousness are operating, stimulus/response, intentionality, thoughts and feelings, there is also awareness that it is I, myself, who am conscious. In the absence of a shared language, it is not possible to be sure that any other animals possess this knowledge, although a few demonstrate behaviour that suggests they might to some degree.

The biologist, Stephen Jay Gould[1] said of consciousness, 'Consciousness is the greatest invention in the history of life; it has allowed life to become aware of itself[2]'. One of the most elusive of all human conundrums is how this invention came about and it has been expressed as a question in the following lyrical way: how did the water of our biochemical selves turn into the wine of our self-aware, conscious selves[3]? This mystery remains although, throughout history human thought has produced many inventive solutions ranging from the theological, through the astrophysical and extra-terrestrial, to the mystical and the metaphysical. My personal preference is for an evolutionary account, which has appeal because it lacks indebtedness to the magical and supernatural. The question to address is: how can a constellation of purely physical matter, a random agglomeration of molecules holding themselves together to form an organic and self-regulating individual life form also manifest self-awareness, a feeling of being me and of what it's like to be me?

Since the publication in 1859 of 'On the Origin of Species[4]' Darwinian[5] models applied to human development have gone through various stages of popularity and acceptance. The full impact and implications of the Darwinian proposition is a hard pill to swallow in that it raises the spectre of human insignificance and many have found this uncomfortable. At times these debates have been both passionately and violently expressed with each side demonstrating a ferocious level of intolerance for the truth of the other. As a brief aside and in relation to our enquiry, it is worth noting that the much of the violence that has emerged in opposition to Darwinian views of humanity have stemmed chiefly from a perception of insult to our eminence and grandiosity in relation to the natural world and our moral and material ascendancy over it. The relevance here is that, in my view, it is these very insults to illusions of omnipotence and easy dominion that generate violent revengeful responses.

Darwin himself recognised several difficulties in his proposals. Some of these were resolved through the ascendency of Mendelian[6] knowledge, the understanding of inheritance and later, genetics. Another stumbling block was the lack of fossil evidence for 'transitional' species. If evolution was a progressive and gradual process this evidence should exist. Furthermore, archaeological evidence demonstrated an explosion of new species around 530 million years ago, followed by a fallow period of a further 500 million years. Not what Darwinian predictions would expect to find. In yet another theoretical inconsistency, Darwin himself was said to be 'made sick' by the ubiquity of evidence for altruistic behaviour amongst many species. Again not what theoretical prediction would expect from a process concerned with impersonal, yet ruthless, individual advantage.

These inconsistencies posed significant difficulties in the sustainability and plausibility in theories of evolutionary development although contemporary apologists have proposed further modifications of the theories springing from modern genetics and inferences from observations of animal behaviour. The problem of altruism is disposed of by proposing that group benefit can outweigh individual benefit as is observed in animal social behaviour and therefore altruism could reasonably be selected for advantage to the species as a whole. The mystery of the Cambrian explosion appeared to be solved through the advent of the theory of 'punctuated equilibrium[7]', which proposes that most evolution is marked by long periods of evolutionary stability and is punctuated by rare instances of branching evolution. Furthermore, the capacity to evolve is found not to be constant across all life forms and the concept of 'evolvability[8]' has been proposed. Following developments in genetics, evolutionary theorists have come to suggest that not only does evolvability vary between organisms, but that it is a selectable property. Organisms can acquire through the evolutionary process itself increases in their evolvability, just as they can acquire increases in fitness. Finally, traditional Darwinian Theory proposes that evolution progresses by means of randomly occurring mutations. However, following contemporary genetics theory it is suggested that natural variation also occurs as a result of design characteristics and not solely from mutation. In essence, what is being proposed here is that natural variation, self-reorganisation and recombination, is fundamental to life itself and such variations will also be selected for advantage. In other words, life itself has an undefined self-organising property that will be subject to evolutionary change.

Contemporary evolutionary theory has come up with some ingenious, and convincing, solutions to traditional objections but it remains somewhat conjectural and, like much truth, relies as much on its emotional and aesthetic appeal as its objective veracity. It remains a curious aspect of the quest that emotions run high on both the evolutionist and creationist[9] sides of the debate, each side accusing the other of unverifiable wishful thinking. I have already declared my own preference for an evolutionary model, preferring to relegate models of development based upon design, the mystical, the supernatural or the extra-terrestrial to fanciful imaginings. Therefore, with my own highly subjective personal craving for a particular preference of reality thus revealed and owned, I would like to proceed with a proposal for the emergence and continued existence of human consciousness of the self from this perspective.

One of the characteristics of the human conscious mind is an ability to create meaningful images that enable it to think about and respond to our experience of being alive in the world. An image in these terms is a mental representation of experience coming from any of the senses, or a memory of such experience, or a purely imaginary representation of an object. The third of these, the purely imaginary would include the words and language that we commonly use to process, and make use of, those images. To understand the mechanics of the creation of images appears to me to be essentially a problem of neuroscience but, in practice cannot be so easily divorced from the other core characteristic of human consciousness. When we are thinking, processing those neurologically generated images, the human mind has a capacity to observe itself doing this work. It can, and in normal consciousness quite automatically will, observe itself at work and respond to those observations. When I am hungry, my self-conscious mind simultaneously reflects on this phenomenon from the perspective that it is I who am hungry not simply that my organic being is automatically reacting to a biochemical loss of equilibrium. Hunger is indeed the final result of biochemical loss of equilibrium and it is possible to imagine expressing and resolving the phenomenon, 'I feel hungry' in the absence of an observing 'I' and in a self-less and wordless way – simply as an organic sensation that triggers the organism to behave in a certain way. We might call this an instinctual or reflex response. An 'instinct' in these terms is a biochemical mechanism involving stimulus and response and is not mediated or influenced by the higher brain. It is something that happens without thinking about it, like the beating of our heart or the digestion of our food. The sensory, organic stimulus of hunger will reflexively trigger the person into a series of movements we might call 'eating', and this action may then lead to another wordless, purely organic, sensation that 'I do not feel hungry'. This crucial life preserving function could conceivably be completed in the absence of thought, of words and without awareness that there is a 'self' who is hungry. In other words, it is quite possible to envisage purely organic human life functioning perfectly well without anyone being present. Life has no absolute need for consciousness of the self and indeed, the vast majority of life on this planet appears to do very well without it.

Human life may well have no need of consciousness of the self but, as we experience every day, it has been thrust upon us by the random meanderings of evolution. This particular evolutionary development of reflexive organic consciousness towards a consciousness of the self is inescapable as the human being naturally and spontaneously co-creates a sense of self. The thinking and feeling person has simultaneous awareness of the one who is present, the one who is doing the thinking or feeling. We know that, as well as being present in external time and space, we are also present to ourselves. Along with all the biochemical happenings, which constitute an alive and functioning human being, there is also something that signifies that I alone am both the subject and object of what is happening. What is happening is happening to me. Moreover, due to the existence of memory, we will automatically locate our present experience within the context of the narrative of a particular life and within an uncertain lifespan. This 'something' is essentially what psychotherapists have come to call 'the sense of self'. The capacity of consciousness to expand into a consciousness of the self is of crucial importance when it comes to understanding and approaching in fine detail the psychological and emotional mechanisms of blame, revenge and vendetta.

A 'sense of self' is possibly one of the most commonly used terms in psychotherapy. To have a 'good' sense of self is the Holy Grail that the self-actualising individual seeks for. What do we really mean by this? Do we mean pride in ourselves, dignity, and mastery of our work or environment? Who do we know that has a good sense of self – great men and women of history, spiritual or humanist gurus and religious leaders, celebrities and superstars, individuals who have pursued and achieved fame, fortune and glory? Or, the ordinary man who potters through his life in a spirit of kindness and gratitude, the matriarch of a large and happy family, the artist, the scientist, the psychotherapist? What is a good sense of self made of?

To begin to look at this question we might begin by understanding the ways in which, over a period of 6 million years, the modern human mind evolved and, with it, consciousness of the self. With what follows, I am indebted to the particularly engaging and plausible writings of archaeologist, Steven Mithen[10] and theoretical psychologist, Nicholas Humphrey[11] in helping me to get to grips with this subject, which is as slippery as an eel in a bucket.

The evolution of the human mind cannot realistically be divorced from the evolution of the brain, which in archaeological terms has taken place over a period of around 4 to 6 million years. I think such long periods of time are difficult to envisage and, in the following descriptions, I have not referred to specifics of association between time frames and particulars of development. Enough for my purposes to try and describe an evolutionary process in which the brain, and thereby the mind, of adult humans have developed from a simple uni-functional intelligence and an obliviousness to selfhood, to complex and manifold integrated intelligences that simultaneously produce a feeling of consciousness of the self.

The modern human being is uniquely characterised in nature by an operational consciousness comprising intelligence, emotion and sensation that co-exists with, and is inseparable from, an awareness of 'me'. It is I who am, uniquely and simultaneously, the subject and object of that intelligence. These two aspects of mind (operational consciousness and awareness of self) cannot be functionally separated in people as they exist simultaneously during normal consciousness. As I have said, it is theoretically possible to imagine acting on sensations of hunger in the absence of knowing that you are present to that sensation and action. However, it is very difficult, in ordinary waking consciousness, to experience this. The closest I can imagine would be something akin to a fugue state wherein the person, to all intents and purposes, is sleepwalking through life and unaware of the ownership of that life. Many people are likewise aware of temporary 'absences' when they may have appeared to be safely functioning, even carrying out complex tasks, but have no awareness of it. However, entwined though the twin aspects of human consciousness may be, it is helpful to attempt to artificially separate these two functions in order to better understand the development towards the creation of the modern mind. It will then be possible to explore the implications of how the modern human mind shapes the way that we form reciprocal connections to the environment, to ourselves and to each other.

To begin with, it is possible to describe a plausible model of the evolution of intelligence as manifest in the human brain. Based upon deductions made from archaeological evidence, such as technological and social advances through time, it is possible to discern three stages. Stage one would reveal a mind operating from a single province of non-specific intelligence and using the rules of simple learning from cause and effect in each separate situation encountered. Behaviour stemming from this non-specific intelligence would be situation specific and generalisation from the particular to other similar situations would not occur. For example, learning that a fruit tree is in a particular location would teach us to return to that fruit tree another day but not to look for other fruit trees elsewhere. Some observers have seen this kind of intelligence operating in very young infants wherein no connections are made across different experiences and no cross-learning occurs.

Stage two of the evolutionary development of intelligence, would see the mind of non-specific intelligence in the first stage becoming augmented by discreet specialised intelligences, each of which would be geared to a specific province of behaviour essential to survival. Such specialised intelligences would be more sophisticated than the first stage intelligence in that they would be capable of generalising learning and perhaps extrapolating within their sphere of concern. For example, it would be of evolutionary advantage to develop more specialised and sophisticated intelligences related to the natural world and to social, technical and linguistic intelligence. Within these specialised provinces it would be possible to learn quickly and modify behaviour accordingly although, at this stage, the specialised provinces do not communicate with each other. That is to say, specialised intelligence about tool making is not appropriated to the province of nature-based or social intelligence. Thus, for example, a high degree of learned skill with tool making will not necessarily translate to more sophisticated group hunting technique, or methods of hunting specific animals.

The third stage of evolutionary sophistication does indeed concern itself with such integration and exchange. Doorways of communication open between the basic non-specific and the specialised provinces of intelligence enabling learning and behaviour modification to proceed at an exponential rate compared to simple situation-specific, isolated learning. Experience gained in one province can be employed by any, or all, of the others giving rise not only to vastly more adaptable and successful behaviour but also to new possibilities in the ways of manipulating thought. The crucial significance of the third stage, integrative intelligence, is that it is this aspect which enables figurative thought. Furthermore, the third stage evolution of the mind generates not only the ability, but also a significant automatic preference, for metaphor, analogy and figurative thought. The language of any integrative system is, of necessity, figurative and through this language, the mind begins to think about itself, within and amongst itself. This automatic preference for metaphor and analogy, to view some things as standing for other things and some things as being like other things, sets the stage for what we might define as distinctively human. Leading to outpourings of creative imagination and the development of language, art, religion, science and technology. Here, we can see the origins of all that is so magnificent, and so appalling, about ourselves.

To employ my own capacity for metaphor for a moment, it becomes possible to envisage these stages in a different way. The first stage would be analogous to individual instrumentalists playing a single tune in parallel, unaware that those around them are other musicians and having no concept of unison, let alone harmony or counterpoint. The second stage is like a suite of practice rooms wherein each musician is a virtuoso, being able to perform a range of styles and even to improvise simple lines. Such musicians have a vague awareness of their neighbours in the next room but it doesn't occur to them to form and ensemble. In the third and final stage, we can picture the modern mind as a constellation of a vast repertoire of highly specialised and skilled individual instrumentalists being wholly aware of each other and of their commonality of purpose operating in harmony, in counterpoint and towards the ultimate service of the whole. We could go on to imagine that the development and adaptive advantage of this group being enhanced by the chance arrival of a maestro, leader and conductor, to unify and integrate the individual and ensemble players as they work. The maestro thereby brings cohesion and identity, a monolithic feeling of selfhood. It is the emergence and (evolutionary) selection of the maestro that could generate the unified self-consciousness, the feeling of what it's like to be the whole orchestra.

I think it is reasonable to propose that here we might see, through a model based on natural selection, the possibility of intelligence beginning to become aware of itself simply through the random selection of naturally advantageous imperatives operating within a complex and interactive mind.

The second aspect of the evolution of the mind, which can be shown to support the emergence of a mind that knows itself, is a consciousness of the self that develops out of organic sensation or simply: what it feels like to be alive. I think that the directly felt, sensory, experience is both the basic building block of any selfhood we might achieve and probably the most useful vehicle for reflection upon that selfhood. I have no argument with the validity of intelligence, and language, as a means of defining, signifying and manipulating meaningful experience but I am reluctant to place it at the root of consciousness of the self and the consequent values of selfhood. Earlier in this chapter I described how self-esteem emerged primarily out of sensory awareness and only secondarily given cognitive form following the development of organised intellect and language. I would go further here and propose that all aspects of awareness of the self, the feeling of what it is to me 'me', likewise emerge first and foremost into consciousness out of sensory perceptions. As a general orientation, I remain someone who sees the essential creation, maintenance and meaning of selfhood as securely located in the realms of the vicissitudes of the body and organic, sensory experience. It is to sensory experience that I will now turn in an attempt to discover how consciousness of the self might have emerged from this.

Sensation, in its most primitive form, is the result of a capacity of an organism to register the presence of elements of its environment. We have seen that this might be either proprioception, exteroception, interoception or a combination of two or three of these. Possibly the more adaptive perceptual mechanism of these three is exteroception as it brings with it the possibility of the organism responding to the environment. Proprioception and interoception give feedback about the state of the organism and therefore, with relevance to our enquiry, are more likely to be implicated in generating the nascent sense of what it's like to be 'me'. The simplest adaptive use of the sensory mechanisms would be a stimulus/response reflex, which does not require anything other than biochemical reactions and certainly not the presence of the sophisticated structures we would call a nervous system or indeed, a consciousness of self. Single cell animals, such as the amoeba, operate in this way and whilst amoebae show features of consciousness in this respect, such reflex-based behaviour is inflexible and does restrict the animal to a very limited repertoire of possibilities other than the maintenance of life. Sensation and response in this respect is functionally one and the same thing. As animals evolved in sophistication, it became possible to identify an increasing separation in stimulus and response and eventually to the structural development of an intervening and mediating function. This organic structure with its simple, meditating function became a place where representations of the stimulus could be registered and, most usefully, where different options might be available regarding a response. It would perhaps be too much to describe this very primitive function as a choice in the way that we might understand the word, but it does provide the animal with a more sophisticated repertoire of responses and therefore adaptive and survival advantage. In the very simplest structures this might only take the form of being able to differentiate 'flavours' of similar stimuli and a variety of possible responses or strengths of response. For example, such an animal would be able to respond flexibly to greater or lesser concentrations of certain elements in the environment. It is known that plants have this capacity in response to certain noxious substances and they are able to respond defensively and appropriately to the degree of threat. Moreover, some plants and trees have the additional capacity of communicating the presence of threat to other plants in the locality and display remarkably sophisticated and flexible responses in this respect. Simple stimulus/response mechanisms thus become flexible and might even be said to be mimicking a very primitive mind.

 A further evolutionary step would be the development of a mechanism for storing responses in order that future responses might become more efficient and here we begin to see the beginnings of a rudimentary memory and a capacity to learn from experience. All of these developments would, most likely be selected as advantageous to the evolution of a more sophisticated, adaptable and thereby successful animal. In the evolution of the human brain and mind we can say that the capacity for stimulus to be 'held in mind', whilst it is processed by degrees of intelligence and whilst choices are made, has given us massive evolutionary advantage. The structures in the human body that this function arises from is nervous tissue and centrally, the brain. It is the capacity of the brain and the nervous system to 'hold in mind' stimuli that create the first inkling of a self. The nascent 'self' might be perceived now as that place within which the stimulus is being held. If it is indeed the case that the consciousness of the self emerges from nervous tissue processing stimuli from internal (body) and external (environmental) sources it would be reasonable to propose that the animal with the largest, most sophisticated and evolved central nervous system would also be the animal generating the highest degree of consciousness of the self. We can imagine that the human being begins to become conscious of this function of 'holding in mind' as an actual place of assimilation and mediation and, through their preference for figurative thinking, to construct images of it. It is not such a grand leap from here to begin to sense such a place as 'me'; as the one who stands between stimulus and response. The state of consciousness develops from an awareness that 'something is happening', towards an awareness that 'something is happening to me'.

A usefully adaptive development of this essentially sensory function is provided by the evolution of a shift in ways of utilising this awareness. Here, the simultaneous development of sophisticated intelligences as previously mentioned, especially the capacity for fusing and integrating individual specialised intelligence and the ascendancy of figurative thought, will be operating in conjunction with the sensory apparatus. In short, it is of enormous advantage if I am able to use the feeling of what is happening to me to answer questions about what is happening outside of me. 'I know the sun is shining because of what happens to me when it shines' can become, 'I know that something is good to eat because of the impact it has on me' can become, 'I know you are a good person because of the way I feel when I am with you.' The conscious awareness of the state of me can become a sign of the state of the environment. Simultaneously, this dual awareness will reinforce the sense of separation between 'me' and 'not me', which is so crucial for the emergence of a consciousness of the self. Hence, the dual nature of consciousness, the subjective and the objective, emerges over time driven by the selective preferences of our evolved nature. The combined complexity and assimilation of sensory and cognitive processes, together with the nascent feeling that there is a 'me' in here and an 'it' out there, propels the individual further into a consciousness of the self. We might say that through the selective mechanisms of evolutionary development and as a result of the developing complexity of their organic structure, the human being functionally (and spontaneously) progressively thinks, feels and acts as if there is someone present to their thinking, feeling and acting.

The most compelling evidence we have for the emergence of a consciousness of the self, other than the purely organic, is the emergence of objects of art. The creation of art can be seen as an act of projecting the 'I' of the self into the environment in order that I, and others, might witness my selfhood. This supposes that the 'I' is significant to the individual over and above purely organic survival. Again, we can see that human beings are alone in nature in creating art in this way and it can be viewed as a direct reference to their awareness of, and a wish to manifest and externally re-state, selfhood, significance and the presence of a person of substance. The first concrete evidence of a consciousness of the self, manifesting as self-import, occurred between 30 and 40,000 years ago with the emergence of representative and symbolic art.

Through the sustained development of a simple intermediary function in the sensory mechanisms between stimulus and response, combined with a massive increase in the cognitive capacities of a more sophisticated, complex and larger brain, the human being has come to behave increasingly as if 'someone' is present to their occupations and endeavours. As a result of this, human beings have come to believe in themselves as creatures of individual and social significance over and above that which a dispassionate evaluation of their organic significance would conclude. The planet earth has been in existence for some 4.5 billion years and for 3.6 billion years has sustained non-human organic life. Such high esteem, dominion and significance we habitually and unquestionably give ourselves is hardly sustainable for a creature who dates its own importance back a mere 40,000 years. However, perhaps it goes some way to understand the hubris and grandiosity which, for around half that time, has a resulted in a documented and wholly unique history of staggering and increasing violence and destruction towards all living things. Having a (misplaced and unjustified) belief in our significance is a defining human characteristic and from this belief materialises everything that is singularly human, for good or ill. Also, born of this belief is the fragile emotional and psychological edifice that remains for ever vulnerable to wounding or collapse in the face of nature, of ordinary human mortality and the natural limits imposed on our desires.

CHAPTER SIX

Self-consciousness begets self-importance begets anxiety

Having taken some time to explore the development of consciousness of the self it is fair to say that, as psychotherapists, my colleagues and I are likely to take consciousness of the self for granted and as a fact of life. Our interest is in the impact that this peculiar fact of existence has on human relationships and especially, the ways in which the life of the emotions are involved. My emotions are my emotions and are recognisable to me as a facet of my consciousness and as significant to my particular life. One question, perhaps quest, thereby becomes: 'is our own consciousness of self a pleasurable experience and one that exists in the absence of pain and anxiety?' I do not ask this question out of romance, or a moral notion of goodness, but from the premise that natural science has shown that life functions best in the absence of pain and anxiety. Adaptive life is, in the broadest of terms, pleasure seeking and pain and anxiety avoidant. The answer lies in the realm of the emotions[1].

Consciousness of the self is central to what it is to be human. Emotional experience is a predetermined and essential element in this and forms the ground that all of our subjectivity, and thereby our sense of personal meaning, purpose and significance rests. It is emotional experience that defines a meaningful life. The feeling, the sensation, of being engaged in a meaningful life is what defines it and not whether my life is indeed, by some rational argument, meaningful. The question: 'How do you know that you are happy?' can be answered in many ways but, only one answer is ultimately satisfying and irreducible: I know I am happy because I feel happy. I have an organically anchored sensation that I have come to name as 'happy'. Answers like '…because I have a new car, a beautiful wife, a satisfying job, and lots of money, fame and glory…' will not actually answer the question. Such answers only beg further questions. How do I know that something is true or that I exist as a person, an individual of significance? The only authentic answer lies in the same realm in that we know and accept beliefs because we experience the emotional truthfulness of them. The core of this emotional experience is the sensory content. Truthfulness is highly subjective in this respect, highly mutable and subject to individual emotional dynamics. Perhaps even in the realm of logical analysis we could say that the solution is the one that passes the tests of proof but also because it is emotionally satisfying. It may well be that the pursuit of truth progresses as much by virtue of a right feeling as well as its rationality. The language of truthfulness, of meaning and of personal significance is the language of the emotions.

I have suggested that revenge has nothing to do with justice; rather it is motivated by an attempt to change an emotional state. Emotional states are the ways in which we know and define the quality of our being, its particular flavour and the relative value of that flavour. They have evolved, like the consciousness of self, from simple organic sensory perceptions and as an adaptive development of the human species. From a biological and adaptive viewpoint, emotional responses are regulatory devices concerned with the survival of the species. In essence, they are a constellation of biochemical reactions to stimuli that result in an integrated pattern of response. Their primary function is regulation of the organism[2]. The emotional response attempts to create circumstances that will be advantageous to the survival of the organism and might be understood as having two elements: firstly, the emotion is attuned to produce a specific reaction to a particular stimulus, such as the familiar fight or flight or freeze response or, to move towards and engage with the environment in response to what we might call desire. Secondly, the emotion is geared to regulate the internal state of an organism in order that it can be prepared for a certain course of action. These twin organic features form an essential part of the homeostatic mechanisms in that external or internal stimuli will, though the intercession of the emotional response, automatically produce a reaction in support of the appropriate survival response. Given the fact of an awareness of the self, it is possible to locate the emotional life as being an intermediary between basic, organic reflex and biochemical survival and the devices of integrated specialised intelligence, reason and thought. It is influenced by both and in turn, informs them both.

Thus far the biological function of emotion might apply to many species of animal and it is fairly clear that many animals have emotional reactions as part of their survival and homeostatic routine. However, as a result of human consciousness of the self and higher intelligences, the human emotional experience is a more complex and dynamic event in that it is also embedded in the narrative structure of an individual life. We have seen that sensation is central to what an emotion is but the human relevance of a sensation/emotion proceeds from the figurative meanings we generate and ascribe to the various elements. External stimulus, sensory perception of bodily changes, reflex and volitional expressive activity, thinking and psychological processes such as memory and symbolic meaning will all contribute to the creation of a narrative meaning for each emotional event. Sadness does not have the same meaning for any two people, nor would anger or joy or terror. Each emotion has a different story and meaning attached to it and each of these will be embedded in the meaning of a person's life. All elements will, within the realm of selfhood, be ascribed a personal meaning and given a qualitative value above and beyond their essential organic function. It is the sensation that is recognised by the intellect and integrated and entangled in the emotion's narrative, thereby giving it a cognitive meaning and value. The simple homeostatic mechanisms of emotion thereby become linked by association in consciousness with the person in whom the emotion is embedded. In this way emotional events become inseparable from notions of value, desire or repugnance, power or vulnerability, attachment or isolation, good and evil and ultimately the meaningfulness of life itself.

The 'sense of completion' in an emotional process is a key to understanding emotional distress in that all emotion stems from a stimulus causes a chemical change inside the person. The organic cascade following the biochemical change is what the intellect will eventually recognise and name as a distinct emotional state. This will be very familiar to all of us and is generally experienced as a discomfort, disequilibrium or restlessness that leads to a desire for expression of some kind. In the healthy state, this desire would generally be indulged and expression through action or movement will naturally follow. Equilibrium will be regained at the completion of the full emotional event. Every emotional event has an organically determined beginning, middle and end. If, however, completion is interrupted then a return to equilibrium is denied and will be felt as distress or anxiety. As the core of the emotional experience is cognitively irreducible, in that it is reflexive in nature and subject to autonomic self-regulatory systems it will, like all reflex mechanisms, embrace a pre-determined pathway that it will attempt to complete. The pre-determination follows the evolved functional organic process. The core of the emotional response is therefore designed to operate within, and be subject to, homeostatic principles and what we call the 'feeling' of an emotional event is sensory perception of these somatic processes. This is how grief can be said to 'hurt' or joy to 'tingle', how rage can feel 'hot' and terror might be 'cold'. The sensory content of the emotion is the closest we might get to a shared experience of emotion, prior to mediation by the individual narrative. For each core feeling there will be a corresponding, and species specific, somatic constellation of biochemical, mechanical and neural changes. That these changes are then mediated by individual self-consciousness, memory and intellect makes each corresponding emotion a subtly different experience and represents a different meaning for each individual. Thus, in the human being, there are two levels of emotional experience: the visceral, being mediated through the evolutionary and organic, and the imaginative, being mediated through personal and cultural narrative, intellect, language and figurative thought.

Therefore, I would define a complete emotional response as a highly complex event that can be usefully understood only from a personal perspective. There is a personal point of view to an emotion that is essential to its full understanding and personal significance. Human emotion, and its relational consequences, can only really be understood if it remains embedded in the narrative of a particular life. Thinking, reflecting and talking about my emotion, and the emotions of others, will be from the point of view of an experienced and creatively self-conscious person who is also capable of thoughts and feelings, and one who has a capacity for literal and figurative reflection on those emotions. Furthermore, it will be from the point of view of an individual who has created their own personal value system related to emotional experience. For example, when I say 'I am afraid' this cannot be said to equate with 'you are afraid'. The physiological response may be similar, qualitatively though probably not quantitatively, but the personal experience and meaning of fear cannot be claimed to be the same. For every emotional phenomenon there will be the person's corresponding narrative structure and it is the pervasive influence of the narrative structure that will define and colour the individual meaning of the emotional event. The sensory content of the emotion can lead to a collective human empathy, whilst the entangled narrative structure makes it unique. Additionally, as has already been said, the person will also have feelings about the feelings. It is these feelings about feelings that are so important in understanding all neurotic states and, in particular, the content and trajectory of the revenge scenario.

If we are to try and understand an individual's emotional response from the point of view of 'why' of such an emotion we will find ourselves in very deep water indeed and, of necessity, need to know a great deal about that person's unique life and their unique orientation to it. A commonly held point of view is that the ways in which we interpret ourselves and others is rational and normative. The presumption exists that there is something we should feel and, perhaps, do feel in any given situation; that there is a right emotional response to a given situation. We know from experience that this is not the case but the illusion persists, particularly in relation to perceived wrongdoing. Hence, in any review of an ordinary day's news reporting we might read that 'any normal person would feel this way', or perhaps more alarmingly, 'every right thinking person should be outraged by this'. However, closer examination of people shows that this is not true, even though we might wish it to be so. How we respond emotionally cannot be seen in the same light as how rain should fall given the prevailing atmospheric circumstances.

For example, it might be relatively straightforward to find a rationally verifiable measure of empathy, appropriateness and proportionality to the fear response that results from suddenly, unexpectedly, seeing a double-decker bus bearing down on us as we cross the road. However, the fear response we might have upon imagining the same bus or of hearing gossip that our spouse is having an affair is a far more complex phenomenon and would require no less than a full biographical thesis to illuminate and understand. What is interesting in terms of our enquiry is that the greater the degree of distress and anxiety generated by any given situation, the greater it appears is the social imperative for everyone to feel the same way about it. This might be another way of saying that the greater the degree of potential threat posed by a given situation the more violent becomes our need for a collective and monolithic emotional response. This is precisely the kind of enforced collectivism that the revenger demands and can be seen as a psychologically primitive way of combating nuance and ambivalence that might otherwise cloud the issue and render the psychological manoeuvre ineffective. As the revenger descends from grey to black and white they will insist that we all do the same. As we shall see in Chapter 8, once the revenge scenario is activated, for sound psychological reasons there is absolutely no space for anything other than a black or white, good and evil view of the wrong that need to be avenged.

Emotional experience has the characteristic of being intentional. It is always 'about something' and in this way emotions are aggressive in nature; they drive towards and attach to an object either in the world or in our imagination. When we have an emotion, we are engaging with real and imaginary objects and people, including ourselves. When we feel fear, there is something that we are afraid of and it is ourselves who are afraid. Even if the thing is a nameless thing it remains a thing. As already mentioned, the 'intention' of the emotion might be discovered through an analysis of a unique life story as well as instinctual and learned beliefs and desires. To take my previous example: in addition to the organic response, it is possible to understand my response to the bus in terms of beliefs and desires. I believe the bus will collide with me, I believe it will harm me, I have a desire not to be harmed and thus the emotional event and response might be intelligible, appropriate and proportional based on a rational, normative analysis. However, the second example (my spouse having an affair) could not be understood in the same way as it is very unlikely that any two persons would have the same emotional (narrative) response to this situation. The personal meaning of our partner having an affair would need to be factored into any analysis.

There is yet another complicating element introduced as a result of the sophistication of human consciousness and this is the idea of having feelings, not just about the objects involved, but also towards the objects involved. Feeling 'towards' something (or someone) might be defined as 'feeling whilst also thinking about and having a personal investment in that thing (or person)'. If the thing or person towards whom we are having feelings has importance to us in some way then this will generate a more complex set of emotions. For example, we might be afraid that I cannot possess this thing or that if we do possess it, we may subsequently lose it or it might disappoint us. How important is the having, or not having, to my thinking well of ourselves? Do we want the thing or do we need the thing? In what way do we need the thing? Constellations of emotion, and relative levels of intensity, will arise depending on our personal narrative and the constitution of our good enough self- image. Should we not get the thing we desire, people might see that we are not master of our domain and thereby, fear of shame and humiliation may arise. The 'matter' here has become of social significance, of concern to self-esteem, and not solely about having, or not having.

Here, we are a long way from simple, self-regulatory concepts with regard to human emotional responses and into very sophisticated notions of self-regard, community and social engagement and attachments to, desires for, specific objects or people. For example, desire brings with it the possibility of states of loss, humiliation and powerlessness and can be drivers for massive anxieties. Desire implies what we know from everyday experience: that people seek attachments, relationships and intimacy with specific others over and above what might be explained by simple homeostatic principles. These relationships are established and maintained fundamentally, not by rational imperatives, but by emotional ones. They will be mediated not only by organic and reflex mechanisms but also by socially mediated learning and the influence that learning has had upon an otherwise self-regulating system. They will also be profoundly affected by, and have an effect upon, our consciousness of ourselves as it is reflected in learned degrees of self-esteem. How we have come to feel about who and what we are will influence everything else we feel towards the objects and people in the world as we swim in the sea of relational experience.

If we can accept that emotional responses are essentially self-effecting, self-regulating, and self-determining then we might wonder why our everyday experience is that our emotions often are the source of a great deal of distress and unhappiness. To put it simply, how is it that my emotional reactions no longer appear to be solely a self-regulating response to specific and limited environmental events but have a life of their own, for good or bad? The answer to this lies in the sphere of the various psychological theories of neurosis that state, very simply, that the self-regulating function of emotional response can be undermined, hijacked and overwhelmed, by life experiences that have interrupted the organic responses and prevented them from fully functioning. More specifically, during some of the circumstances of socialisation, the child's upbringing, the self-regulating emotional response can become distorted through environmental conditioning and in such a case the whole edifice of the emotional response will suffer a corresponding distortion. Depending upon the particulars of the conditioning, and the resulting distortions, the person will grow up to find that they have more or less subjective feelings of pain and anxiety in different areas of their emotional lives and correspondingly, great difficulty with self-regulation.

For example, my own father was a fairly traumatised man who as a consequence had a very low tolerance of excessive noise and movement. His characteristic response to such excess was violence either in ill tempered attack or more usually, sudden withdrawal (to his shed in the garden). The atmosphere and unspoken message he left in his wake at such times was that someone had done something terribly wrong. Having three sons is no way to create a noise and movement free environment. Because my father could not bear it, natural ebullience, play fighting and demonstrative expressiveness of any kind became a source of conflict and distress in the household. Nobody was doing anything wrong but the result was a chronic repression of liveliness in his children. Repression that eventually produced three very well behaved, very nice, boys but with an underlying anxiety, depression, thinly veiled passive aggression, resentment and a generally negative and pessimistic outlook. The suppression of joy can truly make us sick at heart.

Since Sigmund Freud, and the beginnings of the psychoanalytic project, there have been many successful attempts to identify, conceptualise and define what I have called 'conditioning, and the resulting distortions'. There have also been equally successful developments of therapeutic intervention that have attempted to remedy theses distortions and the adverse effects they have on human relationships. It is not my intention in this book to review these attempts, except where they become significant to the particular subject of revenge. Suffice to say that as a profession, analysts and therapists since Freud have produced a plausible and generally effective response to the problems of socially generated human pain and anxiety, unhappiness and destructiveness.

It is an inescapable fact of modern human everyday existence that we are vulnerable to emotional distress and our language and popular culture has developed to reflect this. It is all too possible to feel bad and, given the prevailing cultural and individual values, it appears that some feelings are worse than others. Conditioning of emotional response results from the fact that some emotional states will be allowed in society, even to be encouraged, whilst others might be actively discouraged or attract punishment. This in itself produces a culturally mediated distortion of the organic self-regulatory mechanisms as people will generally seek social acceptance over overt emotional authenticity. For example, 'big boys don't cry' or 'nice girls don't spit' might just produce such well socialised adults, but difficulties will arise when those same big boys feel like crying or some nice girls want to spit. When this particular big boy feels like crying I tighten my belly and jaw, hold my breath and wait for the moment to pass. An effective, humiliation avoiding, technique learned many years ago in the playgrounds and grammar schools of an isolated sea-side town in northern England. It is a testament to the power of such conditioning, and to the relentlessness of the repressed emotion attempting to complete its organic destiny, that to this day I do not cry as easily as my organic self might implore me to, and suffer the corresponding somatic discomfort as a result.

The crucial and relevant thing about this little example is that to this day I carry an organically structured resistance to crying. My self-regulatory mechanisms were overwhelmed and distorted by painful social experience. Neurotic restructuring has embodied the repressive historical situation. This is what psychotherapists would call a 'repressive' manoeuvre, structurally pushing down a feeling with muscular contraction. It is socially adaptive, aimed at maintaining good standing in a particular culture and ensuring that self-esteem remains intact. The price for this is an uncomfortable organic restriction of self-regulating mechanisms and chronic anxiety related to the possibility of the emotion breaking out. Anxiety, in these terms is not an emotion in itself but the side effect of an emotion attempting to self-regulate and being stopped from doing so by somatically embedded learned social responses. The cure for anxiety is therefore theoretically very simple but, given the tenacity and power of our conditioning, not so easy to achieve. This is the very mechanism wherein we can begin to understand that holding on to our feelings can make us physically ill. It has been well understood for some time that 'stress' makes us sick. What 'stress' is in this sense is nothing less than the emotional, and thereby organic stress, which is directly caused by unexpressed, unresolved, incomplete emotional states. When we stop, interrupt or otherwise divert our emotions we are interfering with our fundamental homeostatic mechanisms. This is not sustainable nor compatible with health. We may learn resilience when necessary but, for sustainable health, it is important to understand what this actually entails and to incorporate self-regulatory principles as well. Many a sick person are they who have learned resilience too well and foregone self-regulation.

Given their organic nature, if we attempt to arrest our emotions they cannot be erased and will remain for evermore pushing, seeking completion and causing anxiety symptoms. The result of this pushing is felt primarily as anxiety and will lead to any number of manoeuvres and symptoms whose aim is to find a compromise between the demands of the body for self-regulation and the demands of self-esteem and social acceptance. This is the very essence of neurosis. Every attempt at repression is an incomplete repression and the consequence will be paid in emotional discomfort as a compromise has to be struck in order to reconcile the two conflicting needs. The primary symptom of the neurotic compromise is anxiety. The extent that such compromises are individually and socially successful or individually and socially disastrous will dictate the degree that the person might be viewed as emotionally and psychologically healthy. The compromises we make as children between the conflicting demands of family, and other social encounters, and the claims of organic self-regulation will be implanted in adulthood and pervade all realms of the self in emotional, cognitive and physical structures. They will dictate our characteristic way of being with ourselves, in relationship to others, and to a very large extent the degree to which we will experience life as a thing of ease and contentment or of misery and disappointment.

We have seen that this situation is inescapable in any culture that embraces authoritative hierarchy and obliges any degree of psychological and emotional submission, and thereby a necessary distortion of naturally occurring organic self-regulation. In chapter 4 we saw that both psychoanalytic and social theorists accept the need in all complex cultures for some degree of individual submission and therefore counselled the tolerance of a corresponding degree of emotional repression and inevitable neurosis. The degree that this is necessary is a matter of prolonged and vociferous debate amongst anyone whose interest lies in the sphere of emotional wellbeing and particularly those concerned with child rearing practice as a means of implanting cultural norms to the next generation. It is not necessary to debate this question here except to remind the reader of the concept of excess, or surplus, repression that occurs in the service of human power drama, as opposed to that required simply for agreeable community life to flourish.

In the last few chapters I have described a species of animal of extraordinary mental, psychological and emotional complexity. An animal for whom the facts of existence, and their corresponding evolutionary advancement, has provided it with great adaptive advantages and some perplexing challenges. An animal that, alone in the world, has an acute and ever-present sense of consciousness of themselves as a significant individual. An animal endowed with intellectual and self-reflective abilities, language skills and an aptitude for metaphorical and figurative thinking far beyond anything occurring elsewhere in nature. All this, together with an emotional responsiveness that has developed from a simple self-regulatory apparatus into a complex, flexible and highly adaptive and effective means of reacting to themselves, to others and to the environment in general. Human emotional capacities have further developed to be a means of establishing and defining not only relationships with others but also the relative value and importance of those relationships and within this, the meaningfulness of life itself. A quite astounding animal and with the potential for such mastery of itself and its environment it might be difficult at first glance to appreciate just how anxious this animal is and the extent that its thought and actions are driven by a desire to reduce this astonishing anxiety. Human beings, for all their powers, do not feel safe in their environment. They will devote enormous amounts of time, money and very scarce resources creating a subjective, but verifiable, feeling of safety in all areas of their life. It is an anxiety that far exceeds that required for simple organic survival. Indeed, I would say that this is the defining characteristic of the human condition and stems almost exclusively from the development of a consciousness of self. That the human animal so regularly, and so readily, resorts to innumerable kinds of violence suggests a degree of fearfulness and vulnerability that is difficult, on the face of it, to understand. Despite our remarkable capabilities and potential for easy dominion over the rest of nature it does appear that we are an animal who is, for the majority of the time, very frightened indeed. Human beings see threats wherever they look and imagine threats where they don't look. Perhaps the greatest tragedy for all of us is that history shows, time and time again, that in the face of these real and imagined threats we turn against ourselves. This is very hallmark of the human experience of fear: that it leads us to create schism, conflict and destructiveness when the deeper and perhaps more adaptive response would be to establish comfort, union, accord and creativity.

To understand from where this sense of threat comes, and why we are so acutely aware of it, we need look no further than what I have been describing for the past few chapters. Consciousness of the self, together with a complex and self-regarding constellation of intelligence and emotion, has generated a sense of individuality and selfhood within which we experience an illusion of ourselves as having significance and meaning beyond anything that can be sustained by the bare facts of organic life. Given that our significance rests on an illusion and, like Narcissus, we mistake the illusion for the real we remain vulnerable to a shattering collision with the realities of evolved existence. Painfully confronted with these facts of life, we readily resort to schism, violence and revenge. Self-consciousness begets self-importance and from this we have generated our vulnerabilities and terrible fears.

If we are to look again at the bare facts of organic life and archaeological evidence for the significance of man in the universal scheme, we have a bitter pill to swallow. Archaeological evidence, and most tellingly, Darwin and the evolutionary endeavour have demonstrated that although we may well be unique in many ways, we are also like other animals in being simply a temporary standing wave in the drifting sea of genes. For the biologist, Jacques Monod[4], life is an accident that cannot be deduced from the nature of things but, once it has emerged it evolves by the natural selection of random, fortuitous, mutations. The human species is no different from any other in being the result of a throw in the cosmic lottery. This is hard truth for any of us to accept as we wish to believe, against the evidence, in consciously created progress and social and spiritual development of the species. Monod, in proselytising mood, writes:

'the liberal societies of the West still pay lip service to, and present as a basis for morality, a disgusting farrago of Judeo-Christian religiosity, scientistic progressism, belief in the 'natural' rights of man and utilitarian pragmatism. Man must set these errors aside and accept that his existence is entirely accidental. He must at last awake out of his millenary dream and discover his total solitude, his fundamental isolation. He must realise that, like a gypsy, he lives on the boundary of an alien world; a world that is deaf to his music and as indifferent to his hopes as it is to his suffering and his crimes[5]'.

In beginning to understand our essential feeling of vulnerability, Monod's challenge is the first we might face and it is a challenge not so much to our physical survival but to our self-significance and meaningfulness. It is a vulnerability founded on the emotional imperatives of self-regard and self-significance and, ultimately, self-esteem. Secondly, this challenge to self-regard and significance is brought to us not only by the biological facts of our existence but by the emergence of aggressive and violent strivings of human beings against themselves in an encounter with the triple fears of powerlessness, loss and humiliation. In our wish to be other than a 'temporary standing wave in the drifting sea of genes[6]' we are also continually aware of our insignificance and in relationship to others have a tragic paranoid anxiety that they also want what we want and there only so much to go around. As with the conflicts and clashes that will have erupted amongst human beings as populations expanded in respect of physical resources, modern humans are also quarrelling over an illusion of self that they also perceive to be a limited resource. Human beings are chronically anxious about a vulnerable and scarce illusion of self-significance that has become as essential to them as was food, shelter and sex in previous millennia. The revenge scenario is an example of a complex and severely distorted response to this struggle and is established, prosecuted and maintained by severe anxiety and a desire to redeem and re-establish the significance and value of the self.

In the next two chapters I will begin to present a model of emotional vulnerability that will be the starting point of my detailed proposals for the psychological and emotional function of the revenge scenario. This will also provide the theoretical underpinning of suggestions for effective psychotherapeutic interventions. From this, it will be possible to better understand the reasons for the ubiquity and tenacity of the revenge response amongst human beings and the failure of remedies that are based solely upon reason, moral and ethical imperatives and will power.

To briefly re-cap, and in partial anticipation of what's to come in the following chapters, I could state the following: to seek revenge is to seek to impose suffering upon those who have made us suffer, because they have made us suffer. It is an intimate act between the revenger and the person who is perceived to be the one to blame for the original hurt and having the principle aim of re-establishing the self-esteem of the revenger. This is achieved through a transfer of emotional states involving powerlessness, grief and humiliation from the revenger to the perceived offender. The revenge scenario, as I have defined it, can be distinguished from punishment, deterrence, retribution and reparation by the fact of this singular, emotional motivation. The act of revenge is an attempt to violently evacuate an unbearable emotional state from one person and to forcibly insert it into another.

CHAPTER SEVEN

Seeking what is true is not seeking what is desirable [1]

I began this book with the observation that unhappy people commonly translate their distress into a belief that someone's done something wrong. This might be understood as a mistaken attempt to comfort painful and distressing inner feelings. I think we have come a long way in understanding exactly what I meant by this and it has been revealed as a consequence of the combined phenomena of consciousness of the self and the illusion of self-significance. In this chapter I want to convey my own personal objections to the revenge scenario and propose alternatives based upon psychological imperatives, not ethical or rational ones. I will make a case, based not upon pacifism, faith, rationality, or ethical considerations but upon the assertion that, from a psychological and emotional perspective, the thing we are attempting to gain from the revenge scenario cannot be achieved in this way. The revenge scenario is a massive instrumental error of tragic proportions. The amount of time, energy, excess aggression, boundless misery and destruction it invokes are ultimately fruitless. Furthermore, as that which feels wrong, it irrevocably condemns us all to an eternal carousel of perilously brittle and anxiety-laden lives.

Human beings are remarkable animals yet, like other animals, remain vulnerable to the vicissitudes of nature and must attend to threats to their survival. Through technology and agriculture they have been largely successful in this challenge, although not so willing to share this success equally amongst themselves. In spite of this, they remain vulnerable and due to the combination of consciousness of the self and remarkable intelligence, they are all too aware that they are vulnerable. In particular, I have described how this awareness is translated, though the creation of an illusion of self-significance, to anxiety about the survival of self-significance. For example, if I am caught in a burning building I will try to escape and survive, as would any other living animal present. However, the reasons for my fear and desire to escape will extend beyond a concern for my physical survival or to avoid injury and pain. As far as we can know, the rats in the basement of the burning building will run to escape physical injury or death, being propelled by an emotional response to the fire that will, organically, both motivate and equip them to flee. Unless we subscribe to the Walt Disney view of nature, it is unlikely that the rats will be thinking of the significance of themselves, their lost futures, their past, and their families and loved ones or any other element relating to the sense that they as individuals signify meaning and value. On the contrary, if I am caught in the fire and my life is in danger, I will be anxious with regard to the loss of 'me'; the historical, social and existential significance of 'me'. My panic will be made all the more acute through the fact of its being enmeshed in the narrative of a significant life, a life that matters beyond the purely organic.

Through the random meanderings of evolution, perhaps together with the unexplained tendencies of organic life to self-organise, the modern human being has emerged as a species of animal that experiences itself as having individual value and import. In consequence, there has come to pass a weighty and unavoidable fly in the ointment of what might otherwise be a convivial, masterful and pleasurable existence. This is the recognition that, for reasons both natural and socially created, we have great difficulty accommodating the bare facts of biological existence, the illusion of self-significance and a life that is free of anxiety and dread. In the face of anxiety we have an inclination to descend into states of dread and employ various psychological manoeuvrings, evasions, schisms and hostilities, which commonly result in exceptionally destructive behaviours. It seems that we do not face the facts of life without anxiety and consequently have chosen to resort to enmity of one form or the other. As a result of our unique mind and social arrangements we are particularly vulnerable to, and fearful of, emotional states that have a corrosive effect on our self-significance and social esteem. We do not like to feel that we are, or may be seen to be, impotent, humiliated and grief stricken. In other words, we have great difficulty in facing the awful truth of our insignificance and vulnerability. It is during life events when these emotions may end up landing on our psychological doorstep that the fervent inclination to resort to aspects of revengeful thought and action become strongest. As someone who has worked in conflict resolution for many years I am aware that the rational desire for a 'fair deal' is most commonly undermined, and is stalled, by a much stronger irrational desire to avoid feelings of impotence, humiliation or loss. That the irrational desire often goes unnoticed, denied or unremarked only serves to make it all the more pernicious in its subversion of any progress towards accord and resolution.

As everyday experience teaches us, a lot of people do a lot of bad things a lot of the time and get away with it. It is important to ask the question: what should our response be to those who do us harm? Sociologists, ethical philosophers, politicians, criminologists, theologians and humanists have a lot of helpful things to say on the subject. This is particularly true of deterrence, retribution and reparation. However, I think I have made it clear that I believe there is a core to the impulse to revenge that is also concerned with attempts to control painful psychological and emotional events. This is particularly so when we see attempts by the revenger to control these events in order to bring about emotional comfort and equilibrium following injury or insult. I have intentionally named revenge as being an 'impulse' here in order to differentiate it from a 'drive' in the traditional psychoanalytic sense of the word. There is some disagreement about the actual meaning of this term. The German word Freud used was 'trieb' that literally means 'drive' and not 'instinct'. The impulse to revenge is not a drive (nor, for that matter is it an instinct) as it does not derive its energy solely from the demands of the body in the way that the true Freudian drives do. A 'drive' is part of our basic survival structure, is unadulterated aggression, unaffected by civilising social concern and will operate purely in the service of immediate individual needs. It would generally be regarded as alarmingly primitive when unmodified and a young child having a raging temper tantrum would be an example of a drive showing itself in its pure and unmediated state.

In contrast, the impulse to revenge derives its energy from secondary psychological mechanisms that develop after, and out of, the biological essence. According to psychotherapeutic theory, the 'ego' is that part of the psychic makeup that is concerned with mediating between the needs of the drives and the needs of the person in relation to socialisation and establishing and preserving self-esteem. It might be most easily described as a 'reality tester', and will mediate and guide the person towards adequate, and socially acceptable, selfhood. The impulse to revenge, whilst it does make use of the most primitive of elements of the self and the energy of the drives, might be seen more correctly as an 'ego instinct'. These have been ascribed latterly to Freud's work and they are concerned with relational (social) survival needs and their function is predominantly self-preservative and self-soothing. The impulse to revenge serves just this function: it is self-soothing in the wake of intolerable emotional states. The wrong, insult or hurt, gives rise to intolerable emotional states, at the core of which is a feeling of powerlessness and terror stemming from the devastating awareness that 'I can be hurt'. This flooding of intolerable emotion leads to a shocking fragmentation of the sense of mastery of the self. The generation and prosecution of revenge promises reconstitution.

The crucial role played by aggression, and specifically rage and hatred, in maintaining a sense of psychic stability has been well documented. The psychoanalyst, Robert Stolorow wrote in 1986, 'rage and vengefulness in the wake of injuries…serve the purpose of revitalising a crumbling but urgently needed sense of power and impactfulness[2]' and, Henry Krystal, in 1978, wrote of the defensive value of aggression, to the point of creating an 'affective storm[3]' during an attempt to avoid states of psychic helplessness. Hatred is self-soothing and stabilising, it holds us together when we might otherwise fall apart in the face of our ordinary human vulnerabilities.

Earlier in this chapter, I wrote that for 'reasons both natural and socially created, we have great difficulty in accommodating the bare facts of biological existence with a life that is free of anxiety and dread.' Naturally created difficulties arise as we attempt to reconcile the indisputable but uncomfortable organic facts of life as they collide with our need for human significance and safety. This collision has a tendency to create anxiety of one form or another and presents us with some perplexing emotional challenges. This first, natural, reason for disquiet has been variously described and is best known in established psychotherapeutic theory as the 'givens'[4], the natural facts of human existence. I think of them as the awful truths of life and they are described and discussed hereafter in this chapter. The second potential source of human distress and discomfort is a particular constellation that develops in the human psyche as a result of our collective emotional responses to the first and is dealt with in the next chapter.

In respect of the subject matter of this book, probably the most interesting and relevant thing that can be said about the 'givens' is this: although they have the potential to cause enormous distress and suffering, they are not, in themselves wrong. They are doing nothing wrong, they are just being what they are, and yet we sometimes rage against them as if they were a personal affront to our honour, our dignity and our very lives. Just as there is no essential correlation between that which we wish for and that which is; nor is there any correlation between feeling yourself to be wronged and actually being wronged.

The 'givens' of human existence have been described in several ways in the edifice that is psychotherapeutic theory but possibly most concisely contained in the model known as the existential approach. The significance of the model is that it confers significance and central importance to the unavoidable anxiety that is a natural and irredeemable response to several facts of life. Further, as it views anxiety as a natural state accompanying consciousness of the self, it views anxiety as something to be accommodated and not avoided or repressed. In other words, the presence of anxiety does not mean that something is wrong nor, as we have so dangerously seen, that uncomfortable and distressing feelings of anxiety mean that someone has done something wrong. As maladaptive responses to anxiety can lead to immeasurable hostility and destructiveness this novel and creative approach, and the alternatives it proposes to managing anxiety, has a great deal of merit.

Each of the 'givens' is less a challenge to biological survival and more to the survival and maintenance of self-significance, as born in the midst of consciousness of the self. In the same way that Jacques Monod reminded us so forcefully in the quotation given in chapter 6, the bare facts of life are anathema to self-significance. They are at odds with the emotional and psychological needs of a self-conscious, self-aware and self-important individual grasping at illusions of significance, hopes of permanence and above all, the desire to be 'somebody'. The 'givens' of life are felt as a threat to our self-significance. The way that we confront and accommodate this threat will dictate to a large extent both our sense of ease in being alive and the amount of anxiety-driven injurious behaviour we might engage in throughout our lives.

There has always been a degree of romance and grandiose heroism attached to the existential quest to encounter the 'givens', as if they were a mythological beast that must be valiantly faced and defeated. Indeed, many writers on the subject use the language of the quest and write of courage and fortitude, hardships to be endured, torments to be faced, sacrifice and conquest. There is a more than a little hubristic posturing at times amongst those who claim to be on the quest to face the bare truth of existence. In his writing, the existential philosopher, John-Paul Sartre appears to me to be suggesting many times that inauthenticity is akin to cowardice. In any event, a narrative account of the 'givens' does remain a potent reminder, and a helpful way of thinking about, our essential psychological vulnerability and the imminent menace of anxiety and dread. Existential theory would propose that each of the 'givens' presents the person with an insolvable dilemma which, like all dilemmas, can only be reflected upon and lived with as best we can. To echo the earlier example regarding generation of excess, or surplus aggression, there is a degree of inevitable anxiety inherent in the 'givens'. However, experience shows that the relative amount of anxiety and harm that can result from this anxiety may be moderated following the work of accepting and not fearfully denying them. Denial of the 'awful' facts of life can only be achieved by a splitting of consciousness and psychological wisdom teaches that all splitting of this kind results in degrees of excess aggression. Excess aggression, as we have seen, is most commonly expressed in ways that are destructive to the self or others. There is a general certainty in all therapeutic endeavours that what is split from consciousness will lie in the shadows of our awareness. It will be destructive both to the degree that it remains hidden and the degree to which it must remain hidden. The alternative is to allow that the 'givens' result in unconscious or atavistic anxiety and the negative impact of this on ourselves, and on our relationships, might be lessened by a comforting and compassionate self-reflection and accommodation. Once again, as with other forms of anxiety driven human conflict, perhaps emancipation lies in the prospect of turning towards rather than turning against.

The first of the 'givens' is concerned with freedom, responsibility and potency. It reminds us that should we desire freedom and the power to be champions of our own destiny, we must also accept the inevitable responsibility that goes with it. It is possible, through mendacity or accusation, to escape responsibility whilst exercising power but this will have psychological consequences that may find expression through, for example, guilt and anxiety or depression and hostility. The avoidance of the burden of responsibility is commonplace as is, perhaps more surprisingly, the avoidance of freedom. The temptation to take refuge in an attitude of 'not free and not responsible' is remarkably popular. Indeed this is the characteristic stance of the revenger inasmuch as it corresponds with the standpoint of the revenger as victim and therefore reasonably justified and not responsible for that which follows. Existential theory would declare that the 'not free and not responsible' stance has psychological and emotional consequences, and a profound effect on intimate and satisfying relationships simply because it not a truthful stance. It is living a lie to yourself and to others.

Whilst it cannot be denied that our freedoms are limited by circumstance and a corresponding limitation of responsibility must be allowed, it remains that the degree by which we commonly and characteristically evade real freedom and declaim our responsibilities is habitually understated. The existential given here is that we are more free and more responsible than we are generally comfortable with being. The anxiety generated by this 'given' creates the necessity to invent psychological mechanisms grounded in denial which, in turn, limit our capacity for intimate, authentic and non-injurious relationships. An example would be the young man who sits for two hours in traffic every morning to get to a job he despises and tells himself that he has no choice. Whilst this may be true to some degree, perhaps it is also a comforting manoeuvre in the face of his disappointment with himself, in that his life is not what he hoped it would be and perhaps, in truth, this is indeed something of his responsibility. He may well be humiliated, feel powerless and ashamed of himself for not living up to be the man he thinks he should be. It is not so hard to imagine such an unhappy man maintaining very discontented and injurious relationships with his family and friends as he tries to pretend other than what his shame and disappointment tells him about himself. He may well do great harm from his castle in the air whilst attempting to prove he is the kind man he wishes to be, in the face of feeling himself not to be.

The second 'given' is concerned with death and human limitation and reminds us that we have not lived forever and that we will not live forever. That we appear to be less disturbed about the first fact (that we have not lived forever) gives support to the notion that our anxieties are indeed based upon consciously generated self-significance. Contemplation on not-being once we have been seems to be far more disturbing than never having been. Whilst a continual and constant awareness of the fact of our death is probably incompatible with psychological health and vitality, it is also important to live within an awareness of the end of our self-significance and yet, not to be anxious to the degree that absolute denials and psychological schism occurs. As we have seen where a risk to life is imminent, the awareness of death is a severe threat to the importance of the narrative of our lives. In a less acute way than finding ourselves in a burning building there does exist the immanence of death as a given of life and again, the ways in which we accommodate this with relative degrees of denial or acceptance will have a substantial effect on our anxieties and our relationships. An example here might be the middle aged man with three ex-wives and children he barely sees. He professes to value freedom and authenticity, does not have close friends or other personal attachments in the way of meaningful possessions. He prides himself on being a lone wolf. It may well be that such a man is so afraid of loss that he dare not possess anything he could possibly lose; this could conceivably extend to his own life. He has legitimised his way of life through shrewd self-deceit, masquerading as an idealisation of freedom and non-attachment, though perhaps also concealing a chronic and disabling anxiety about his own death and non-significance. I have worked many times with such men and their fear of loss and of death, whilst denied, is overwhelming and disabling.

The third 'given' is concerned with what has been described as 'existential isolation' and reminds us that as individuals we are separate from other individuals and this can never be fully overcome. This is different from the common conception of loneliness although social or interpersonal everyday loneliness might be made all the more terrifying by the resonances it might make with existential loneliness. Confusion between the different kinds of loneliness and isolation may give rise to unhealthily symbiotic relationships as the person strives to avoid the unmanageable anxiety. Alternatively, it may lead to avoidant relationships as the person equally vehemently strives to deny their needs and thus press the fears of separation anxiety out of awareness. The 'given' might be described as a dual awareness that we are dependent beings, dependent on others and on nature for physical and emotional survival, but that we are also separated capriciously, and irretrievably, from those others. The degree of anxiety generated by this 'given', and the ways in which the person might accommodate this anxiety, will dictate the characteristic way they form and maintain personal relationships. It will also dictate to what degree they may find relationships secure and satisfying. An example here could be found in almost any tale of romantic love wherein the belief is that 'we can't live without each other'. The epitome of romantic love, those star crossed lovers, Romeo and Juliet, were so in love that death came to them both following separation. We might see this as the height of the romantic ideal or, as the distorted manifestation of an attachment disorder. The romantic ideal of, 'I can't live without you' might be generated from a misapprehension of the degree of threat in the separation. A misapprehension arising from an unhelpful avoidance of existential fears and not from any realistic measure of the present, actual, threat to individual survival.

The fourth 'given' is concerned with meaning and meaninglessness and reminds us that we are, as a direct consequence of our consciousness of the self, creatures that seek to create a plausible meaning in that consciousness. By plausible, I refer to a meaning that will reduce the anxiety generated by the absence of meaning. Carl Jung[5] taught that man cannot tolerate a meaningless life and the anthropologist, Ernest Becker[6] wrote 'Man cannot endure his own littleness unless he can translate it into meaningfulness on the largest possible level'[7]. The creation of meaning essentially operates within the realm of storytelling, of mythmaking and as we cannot ever know that any meaning is truly legitimate it remains, in essence, a fiction. The real test of validity is perhaps a pragmatic one as to whether the story functions well, or not, as an anxiolytic. Perhaps also, whether or not it can be sustained without needing to resort to behaviour that does harm to ourselves or other people. That is, does my story 'work' in satisfying my emotional need for significance and meaning and thereby reduce my existential anxiety? Secondarily, we might add the caveat: does it work in a reasonably sustainable way in the face of contradiction and what degree might we have to resort to violence of one form or another to sustain it. One common denominator in all human conflict and hostile behaviour is surplus aggression that serves to support the ascendancy of one story over another, contradictory, story. Human beings will readily kill, and be killed, to support a belief in their particular, meaning engendering, stories and myths. In respect of the ability to reduce anxiety, the creation of meaningful stories can be to different degrees, sustainable, verifiable and serviceable. Experience shows that it is extremely hazardous to dispute over which is the more enduring, true or functional in any group of people.

The test, in as far as the current enquiry is concerned, is not whether the story is 'true' but if it is emotionally and psychologically functional. If not, then we should ask how it much it might result in the need for distortion and denials that will incur relational or personal costs elsewhere. On the level of meaning, we cannot truly know anything; we can only choose to believe something and that, because it suits us emotionally to believe it. In these terms personal belief, and with it the truth of the stories we tell, cannot be separated from personal narrative and the demands of emotional and psychological equilibrium and, in particular, the management of anxiety and dread. As an example here we might see how the fundamentalist, the zealot, the revolutionary is in flight from the doubt and emotional pandemonium that might otherwise arise if their beliefs were not held to be so doctrinaire, so bellicose and so undeniably right.

The fifth, and final, 'given' is concerned with the fact that we are emotional beings and reminds us that all the foregoing givens can only be approached through the tinted spectacles of an emotional configuration fabricated from the narrative of our individual lives. We have already looked at the adaptive function of our emotional responses in chapter 6 and it is also true to say that the emotional underpinning of all human experience brings forth the sense that life is either, quite simply, good or bad. Psychologically, there is no objective measure of good or bad, only what feels good or bad to the individual, or a consensus within a group. Rational validation, based on moral considerations, is an advanced and linguistically dependent form of ethics but is essentially founded upon emotional imperatives and emerges from the 'feeling' of right or wrong. I am aware that this is a highly questionable form of ethical validation, inasmuch as many people have done some pretty appalling things and felt good about it. However, it remains a 'given' that emotional necessity, and particularly that of anxiety reduction, is commonly in the ascendant when considering ethics and it is an illusion that we are, first and foremost, rationally impelled. Thus, the 'given' here might be put more simply as pointing to the primacy of our emotional responses in perceiving, valuing and finding meaning in our lives. Cognitive and language mediated rationalisation might well follow from this, legitimising our irrational preferences and providing the sense that what we believe is rationally solid. The 'given' brings a perspective to this attitude and proposes that the truth of our emotional responses, being founded on very early life compromises and our own individual narrative, must be cautiously approached if to be taken as a measure of external, consensual, reality. Our emotional responses are probably not, in the absence of self-reflection, the most reliable and verifiable guide to external, verifiable reality. Furthermore, if our rationality is built upon the shoulders of our emotional experience even our so-called rationality might be called to account. In approaching the challenge of the 'givens' of life it will be important to likewise challenge our own, personally constructed 'givens' and attempt, inasmuch as it is ever possible, to rightly see what we are and what is out there.

The 'givens' of human existence together form a potent source of anxiety, either known or unknown. To the extent that they are known and accommodated they may also require defensive distortions of emotion and behaviour that may cause excess distress to ourselves and our relationships. It has been more than adequately demonstrated that one of the results of ungoverned anxiety is a splitting of attention away from external reality and towards a more comforting internal illusion. In some ways we could say that this is what is happening when we create meaning from our lives in that we take something which is random and unconcerned with individual significance (biology) and invent stories about it in order to create an illusion of order, self-significance and meaning. Illusions are a necessary comfort in an indifferent universe and it is important not to dismiss this necessary constituent of emotional ease and stability. However, it remains vital to also question the amenability, or otherwise, of a particular illusion and the price we may have to pay to maintain it. In the next chapter I will present a plausible model of illusion building, which is based in established psychotherapeutic theory, and lead on to examine differing individual susceptibilities to resorting to the revenge scenario. I will attempt to answer the question: why are some people more likely than others to pursue and extract revenge. The answer to this question can help deepen our appreciation of what the revenge scenario is really about, the reasons for its ultimate failure and to finally introduce real possibilities for a more successful and sustainable response to hurt.

CHAPTER EIGHT

The endless struggle to think well of themselves

'The Cocktail Party', by T S Eliot[1], was first performed at the Edinburgh Festival in 1949. It is the story of an estranged and disaffected couple who, through the vehicle and drama of the play, manage to come to terms with the limitations of their lives and are reconciled to the grim compromise this entails. On a deeper level, it is an exploration of isolation in the human condition and the illusions we create, the stories we tell, in order to cope with alienation. It also documents in painful detail the effect such deceptions have on ordinary human relationships. Desperate harbouring of illusion, self-deception, mendacity and avoidance of reality are central themes in the play. The movement towards truthfulness and coming to terms with the limitations of ordinary life is encouraged by a mysterious stranger, who is later revealed as the psychiatrist to the unhappy couple. At the conclusion of the play, the couple are reconciled to a life that might be seen as hollow and superficial compared to their previous illusions but the author appears to be suggesting that ordinary reality is a superior choice to fantastic illusion. The reconciliation is further facilitated by the martyrdom of the husband's mistress. From a psychological perspective, the surrender of the mistress can be seen as an embodiment of the necessary sacrifice and terrible emotional loss that the couple must face in order to reach a dis-illusioned, but reality-oriented life. Whilst the author perhaps reveals some of his own biographical material, and a stiff morality tale behind the transformation, the play remains a compelling study of the development of relationship from the rigid confines of illusion and self-deception, through sacrifice, dis-illusion and grief and towards ordinariness and reconciliation. It is a journey that will be re-told more closely in the case study in chapter 10 as it is of vital importance in understanding how we might attempt to arrest the ravages of chronic impulses to revenge. In Eliot's play, in a moment of elucidation, the mysterious stranger speaks of the motivation behind the grandiose stories we tell about ourselves and the harm that can arise from them:

> 'Half the harm that is done in this world is due to people who want to feel important. They don't mean to do harm but the harm does not interest them. Or they do not see it, or they justify it because they are absorbed in the endless struggle to think well of themselves[2]'

Storytelling, myth making, and the creation of illusion is possibly the most potent tool we have for reducing the anxiety that is generated simply by virtue of being self-conscious. In the 'endless struggle to think well' of ourselves, the stories we make up and tell about ourselves are of crucial importance. In this chapter I want to describe my thoughts about the relationship between the kinds of stories we make up and tell and the likelihood, or otherwise, that we will resort to thoughts and acts of revenge as a balm when confronted with hurt or distress.

Frequently, it will be found that the stories we make up and tell about ourselves are infinitely preferable to the stories that might be told by a dispassionate observer. Unhappy children are extraordinarily inventive story tellers. Stories can become a refuge and comfort in hard times and in such cases woe betide anyone, well-meaning or hostile, therapist or evangelist, who tries to get between us and our story. What child does not know and love the fairy tale of the poor unfortunate who is secretly the special, chosen one. The one who, after many misfortunes and through fortitude and the intervention of magic and fate, is revealed and finally receives much deserved love, fortune and fame? What unhappy adult does not have a grown up version of the same story to ease and provide balm to a disappointing life? What perplexed and isolated person is not drawn to stories of infinite benevolence and love that lie just beyond the present daily experience and may be had simply by virtue of believing and keeping faith with the story? In each instance belief in, and fidelity with, the story is the only requisite demand of the magical promise to eventually deliver a soothing miracle, in whatever way the story is calculated to deliver it.

Storytelling is unquestionably a necessary part of emotional health as who could stand to face the starkest of 'givens' in the absence of some promise either of salvation or meaningfulness within it all. Salvation springs from our intellectual and figurative capacities in the form of myths and stories that provide respite and security from the potential ravages of meaninglessness, overwhelming anxiety or, more prosaically, a forlorn childhood or a disappointing adulthood. Moreover, they can be stories and products of imagination that, unlike real life, the storyteller is creator and master. Mark Twain[3] wrote that 'reality can be beaten with enough imagination', and more famously, T. S. Eliot, 'humankind cannot bear very much reality'. The novelist, Shirley Jackson[4]: 'no live organism can continue for long to exist sanely under conditions of absolute reality'.

It seems that even in the best of world's pure, organic, reality is something that requires a fair dose of storytelling to make bearable. When we look at psychotherapeutic theory we find that this predisposition to make up, tell and uphold stories about ourselves and our environment has long been recognised and documented. The function of storytelling is emotionally and psychologically protective, in that the story will re-describe reality in a way that is both comforting and meaningful to the storyteller. Furthermore, the story will attempt to re-describe the storyteller's experience in a way that enables the storyteller to cope with that experience. Thus, we find Cinderella amongst the ashes comforting herself with stories of mysterious princes and secret discoveries of real and loving parentage. This is something that we all do, to different degrees and in response to different degrees of environmental distress. It is a uniquely human response to existence and makes life more bearable, more interesting, creative and ultimately more meaningful. It is a poetic response to life whereby aesthetic truthfulness rightly outstrips the objective and verifiable.

However, should the distress or life events be traumatic enough the storytelling may become essential to everyday psychological coping and to a degree that it interferes with ordinary intimate, consensual and healthy relationships. In such a case the storytelling becomes problematic for all concerned and reaches into the realms of narcissism[5]. The concept of narcissism is probably the area of psychotherapeutic theory about which more has been written than any other psychological phenomenon. Prolonged and complex debate continues to this day about nuance but the core function of a narcissistic stance remains one of making, telling and protecting a story about the self that serves to reduce distress and anxiety. It is worth examining this concept in some depth as it is central to a psychological appreciation of the extraordinary tenacity and ubiquity of the revenge scenario.

The term 'narcissism' or 'narcissus-like' began to appear in medical literature in the very late 1800's and was first formalised as a specific psychological dynamic by psychoanalysts Sigmund Freud[6] and Otto Rank[7] in the early 1900's. Freud, in 1905, used the term to account for the object choices of homosexuals in seeking a young man who resembles themselves and whom therefore, they may love as their mother loved them. In 1914 Freud published 'On Narcissism, an introduction[8]' that was a more far-reaching, theoretically developed and plausible account of the clinical implications of narcissism. Freud's close colleague Otto Rank, publishing in 1911, presented the first psychoanalytic paper specifically concerned with narcissism[9]. In this paper narcissism, fast becoming an identifiable pathology, was associated with an excessive preoccupation towards vanity and admiration of the self. A massive undertaking in psychoanalytic research followed these small beginnings, continuing the recognition and understanding of narcissistic processes. The result is that one of the central concerns of contemporary psychotherapy is the endeavour to resolve the ravages of the narcissistic state as it is revealed in individual and group culture. All models of emotional distress and neurosis, together with the commonly found lists of everyday emotional problems that the talking therapies offer to attend to, can now reasonably be subsumed under a common analysis reflecting the degree to which the underlying narcissistic state impacts on them. This is to say that we are rendered more vulnerable to day to day emotional and psychological problems by the degree to which we might be, in common parlance, 'narcissistic'. In the simplest terms, we are much more vulnerable to everyday emotional stress because of the real and ever present danger that the stories we have made up and told about ourselves, the stories that we have come to rely on for security, comfort and well-being, will be revealed in destructive ways to be falsehoods. For example, the normal loss and grief that will accompany the end of a relationship will be that much more difficult to manage in a healthy way if the person involved has previously told themselves stories, and hence built their self-esteem, of how they don't really need anyone and can cope alone in the world. Or conversely, if they have told themselves stories about their great prowess as lovers and partners. These stories will pre-date the current crisis and will probably reflect a much earlier emotional need related to the loss of important people. Whilst the stories may originally have served well in protecting the person from childhood distress, they are now a trap that they cannot escape from. The trap in the first example being an emotional need to maintain a persona of being unconcerned by the loss and therefore unable to seek any comfort. In the second example, an emotional need to re-establish the image as a potent lover and effective partner as quickly as possible. Denial and degrees of anxious manoeuvrings will follow, probably resulting in considerable harm to self and others. Revenge might be just around the corner in such a case as it can further support the need to deny heartbreak or loss or prove that the other was wrong to end the relationship. In each event the purpose of the revenge will be to get the wrongdoer to feel the way we currently feel. To evacuate our bad feelings and force them into the wrongdoer.

The term 'narcissism' is taken from the 2000 year old myth of Narcissus, who was the son of a river god and an exceptionally proud and arrogant hunter. Narcissus was distinguished both by his physical beauty and the disdain he showed towards those who loved or admired him. The story is of his downfall. At the beginning of the story Narcissus is walking in the woods and he is discovered by the mountain nymph, Echo. Echo immediately falls in love with the beautiful young man and follows him. Sensing he is being followed, Narcissus calls out 'who's there?' to which Echo replies, 'who's there?' When they eventually meet Echo is rejected by the arrogant Narcissus and heartbroken. Echo retreats to a lonely life with only the sound of an echo to comfort her. The goddess of revenge, Nemesis, hears the sad story and sets out to punish Narcissus by tricking him to gaze into a pool of water, where he sees his own reflection. He is mistaken in not realising the reflection is just that and, thinking it was another beautiful creature like himself, promptly falls in love. Narcissus remains enchanted by the reflected image, entangled in unrequited love and is heartbroken unto death. Other versions of the story are similar in content, of arrogant and harsh rebuttal of loving advances followed by punishment for such rejection. Some versions of the story have Narcissus committing suicide in response to his final plight.

Narcissism has therefore been described as a pattern of attitudes, character traits and behaviours that coalesce around an infatuation with the self, to the exclusion of others. It is associated with a ruthless pursuit of personal gratification that is undertaken with no regard for the feelings, needs or rights of others. Most descriptions of narcissism accord with each other in these basic characteristics but are generally imprecise in one vital component: the crucial element to note is that the narcissists' infatuation, the obsession and entanglement, is not with the self but with an image of the self. The narcissist is one who mistakes the image for the real and, moreover, prefers the image. Like Narcissus in the story, in our narcissism we prefer the image, the reflection, the story told about the self to the actual self. In extreme states of narcissism the actual self may well be so unformed as to barely exist and, in effect, there is nothing to the person but the image. In this respect, it would be more correct to describe narcissism either as a rejection of the self or a substitute for an unformed self. It is a profound and rigid attachment to an image of something that is not the self but is a more acceptable replacement.

The concept of narcissism provides the link between existential and environmentally generated anxiety, the protective manoeuvre of storytelling and the creation of an illusion of the self that serves to establish and maintain the needs of both personal and social esteem. To think well of ourselves we may come to think that a storybook self is preferable to a reality-based one. However, the price that we and others around us might pay for this orientation can be a high one. It requires considerable emotional and practical effort, often desperate manoeuvrings, to ensure that our view and the view of others remains always, like Narcissus, on the reflection in the lake; on continuing to believe that our constructed myth and the image it contains is real. This effort and the necessary manoeuvrings will have a profoundly destructive impact on any prospect of authentic, intimate and anxiety free relationships. Furthermore, as the maintenance of a narcissistically oriented self involves severe rejection and neglect of any reality-based self the trap deepens because we are unable to view ourselves in any other way. Like Narcissus, so for us: the illusion is an illusion that we do not know is an illusion.

It is important to realise that narcissism, and narcissistic elements of personality, are a pre-requisite to healthy self-regard and functional relationships. As with repression of emotions, as with aggression and as with existential anxiety, so it is with narcissism in that we are concerned with excess or surplus narcissism. Surplus narcissism can be defined as that which is required as a defensive psychological and emotional manoeuvre, necessary to deal with unbearable experience and resulting in distortions to ordinary healthy functioning. Thus, we have a concept that embraces both 'healthy' and 'unhealthy' narcissism. Sigmund Freud had a very appealing hypothesis about these twin aspects of narcissism in that he described a zero-sum economy between the two. That is to say, the more healthy narcissism exists in the personality, the less unhealthy narcissism there can be, and vice versa. He wrote, 'the more of the one is employed, the more the other becomes depleted[10]'. In Freud's theories of narcissism he saw narcissistic processes as a normal part of human psychological development and an essential component in the construction of a healthy self-esteem. A 'primary' narcissism exists from birth and is the motive force behind the desire to survive, the psychic counterpart of the organic drive to self-preservation. In this, it might be seen to be wholly self-directed and unconcerned with external objects, except those objects that impact on the survival needs of the infant. Indeed, most child development theorists describe a very early stage of personality development wherein the infant is unaware of itself as a separate individual. All and everything in their experience is 'me'. The separate and identifiable 'me' in relation to 'you' only develops at a later stage. It is only at this later stage that the infant begins to recognise others as 'not me', by withdrawing their self-boundary to their organic boundary. As this happens a 'secondary' narcissism may develop, which is characterised by an ability to view other people as separate objects of esteem and worthy of love and attachment.

Freud proposed that an unhealthy narcissism will result from interruptions and distortions occurring during the transition from primary to secondary narcissism. The pathological state of narcissism emerges as a result of an unsatisfactory and incomplete transition to the secondary stage and a developmental arrest. The developmental arrest manifests as an inability to accommodate the existence of others as having value in their own right. Following Freud, the Austrian-born American psychoanalyst Heinz Kohut[11] developed the original hypothesis and proposed that primary narcissism is a form of grandiosity and omnipotence and will generate storytelling that is unrelated to reality, but comforting to the requirements of the vulnerable infant and primitive narcissism. Maturation into secondary narcissism and the gradual intervention of a socialisation process will progressively transform grandiosity and omnipotence into self-regard, regard for others and a moderated, reality based, potency. Moreover, the previously held idealised illusions can be used as a skeleton for core moral values and be carried into adult life in much the same way as fairy tales might provide a primitive blueprint for moral behaviour.

As with Freud, Kohut identified that it is when interruptions occur in this developmental process, through inadequate or traumatic child care, that the primitive form of narcissism will persist. In the face of an unsatisfying or frightening environment there will be little to tempt the child out of the solipsistic comfort of primary narcissism. The persistence of primary narcissism and its attachment to naive and brittle stories about the self, renders ordinary human relationships based on mutuality, empathy and affinity almost impossible. In practice, the transition to secondary narcissism and the ability for mature adult relationships is never complete, nor is it constant and unwavering. Archaic elements of primitive narcissism remain in all of us and are likely to emerge at times of distress, anxiety and conflict. Any ominously fearsome crisis in life can make narcissists of us all. Grandiosity, arrogance and omnipotence, disregard for others, anti-social behaviour, magical thinking, envy and entitlement, exploitation and shamelessness lurk in the shadows of the personalities of all people and will emerge at times of stress. However, for many people adequate and loving care giving early in life will mean that a transition to secondary narcissism has been largely achieved and such tendencies are generally held in check by the forces of empathy and compassion, love and kinship and an awareness of the advantages of co-operative mutual dependency. Narcissism is not, therefore, a 'have or have not' character trait but a description of a normally compromised human condition and will show different degrees of presence and consequence in each of us. The degree that we might describe our own narcissism as problematic will be the degree to which it interferes with consensual and convivial relationships and this, in turn, will reflect the degree that each of us has successfully negotiated the transition from primary to secondary narcissism.

Healthy and functional growth and development of living organisms proceed from a combination of genetic predetermination and favourable environmental conditions. Every gardener knows this. This simple combination remains true in respect of human organic growth and development as well as maturation of the personality and the emotional and psychological self upon which ease of living is built. Therefore, the transition from primary to secondary narcissism will not proceed in unfavourable conditions despite the genetic propensity for it to do so. When the development to a secondary narcissism, the re-alignment of focus from absolute self towards self and other, is discouraged by neglectful or traumatic care giving, the process will stall and as has been said already: 'the storybook self is [remains] preferable to a reality-based one'. In psychotherapeutic theory, all persistent and problematic narcissistic features in people would be correlated with failures in care giving, not of genetic predisposition, and thus potentially amenable to therapeutic intervention.

If there is one common feature in the reams of advice and guidance regarding caring for the development of infants and young children it is that it is impossible to get it absolutely right. To take the gardening metaphor a little further, there are some environmental elements that are known from experience to encourage good tomatoes, together with some advice on what will not. However, we are not after prize winning tomatoes. Perhaps a better metaphor would be to see that there are some behaviours and attitudes that will encourage a frightened kitten out from under the sofa, and other behaviours and attitudes that will encourage it to stay hidden. We can reasonably assume that the kitten has a desire to come out and play but, what happens in the surrounding environment will decide the matter one way or the other. I think I have described well enough the precise nature of the kitten we are trying to encourage and, endowed with this understanding and in the light of experience, we can call to mind some strategies that might be successful, and some that might not.

The essential strategy is one of allowing and tolerating what the kitten is, while simultaneously inviting, encouraging and sometimes nudging it towards something that it has not yet become. The simplicity of this essence belies the massive difficulty of the parental task. Difficulties can arise either, because we cannot allow and tolerate the primary narcissism and will be tempted to crush, to humiliate or to punish. Alternately, because we push the infant too forcefully and too quickly into an artificial, unsustainable and fragile maturity. Such difficulties will likely trigger the care giver's primary narcissism to reassert itself. The parent can lose patience, become bullying, punishing and abandoning towards the child, wishing to avoid their own adult feelings of defeat, humiliation and loss. What parent has not struggled mightily with their own self-esteem when confronted with the grandiosity, omnipotence and sheer bloody-mindedness of a determined infant? What parent hasn't entertained thoughts of revenge at these seemingly impossible moments? The task is doubly challenging in that it has to be faced and negotiated twice: once in early infancy and again during adolescence. I will not list the ways in which care giving, parenting, might fall short of being good enough when faced with these profound challenges. These are well known and do not merit another documentary here. Enough to say that neglect, abuse, trauma or more benignly, ignorance, naivety or well-meaning but ill-informed child care practice can all impact adversely on the infants', or adolescents', willingness and capacity to develop out of the solipsistic refuge of primary narcissism. The failure to successfully negotiate this crucial transition has a disastrous effect on the ability to engage in mutually nourishing and sustainable adult human relationships. I have given an example, as a case study, in chapter 10 of one such scenario, the impact on the person's adult life and some possibilities about how this might be approached psychotherapeutically.

I have so far described the interplay between developmental predisposition and environment, and the consequences for both healthy and unhealthy narcissism in the child and adult. From here on in I will use the term 'narcissism' and 'narcissistic state' to refer solely to the immature state wherein undeveloped primary narcissistic elements persist into adulthood. I want to describe two polarities of the narcissistic state as it is revealed in adulthood. Firstly however, we have to try not to fall into the trap of labelling such adult attitudes and behaviours as morally or ethically wrong and therefore, bad. Problematic they may be, sometimes impossible to live with and deeply infuriating but, remember also that the person is not doing anything wrong[12]. The narcissistic response is an attempt to protect a person from something supremely terrifying. The supreme terror is evoked by a movement away from the comfort and refuge of the imaginary self and involves nothing less than a fear of annihilation of what feels to be the whole of the self. For the narcissistically wounded person the illusion is everything that they are. If the illusion is shattered by incursions of external reality then they too are shattered. Any illusion, like a mirror, a reflection in a pond or a portrait in an attic will remain always vulnerable to damage in a way that a reality based, consensual, sense of selfhood will not. As an adult, to be caught in the grip of a significant narcissistic state is a deeply isolating and terrifying experience. The attitudes and behaviours I will describe are both products of immature narcissism and strategies designed to hold at bay incursions of external reality that might destabilise, or destroy the indispensable illusions.

At one end of the spectrum is the flavour of narcissism we are all subject to at times of distress or crisis. At such times there is a tendency in all of us to regress to more primitive ways of coping and a temporary reversal of narcissistic development is very common. We may display intemperance and selfish dismissal of others, grandiosity and arrogance, violence in one form or another and have a general attitude that our needs and desires are of utmost importance and that those of others are trivial by comparison. These attitudes and behaviours might be transient, may be triggered by a stressful life event and we may well feel remorse and express regret at a later stage. I think it is reasonable to propose that we all are capable of such behaviour and in different degrees for each person. Every one of us has a latent and immature narcissism that can be triggered by life events.

Conversely, at the other end of the polarity is the person who displays an extreme and enduring personality distortion that is dominated by the arrested primary narcissism. In such a person reality testing is solely carried out against measures of internal illusion, images of the self and against stories made up and told in the service of denial, withdrawal and avoidance. A narcissistic orientation to life is entirely self-referencing and unable to process or tolerate dissonance with regard to external events. For example, if we need to maintain an image of ourselves as expert in some given subject we will not tolerate any contrary opinion, violently suppress it should it arise, ridicule the person we are in dispute with and generally resort to pugnacious belligerence. In such a person stressful life events will further exacerbate the defence. Rather than being capable of modifying, toning down or 'owning up' to the stories, the person is likely to increase their grandiosity, omnipotence and disregard of reality to the point of total disassociation. Prejudicial attitudes commonly belong in this category. It has been demonstrated that the more the prejudice is confronted with verifiable, contrary, facts the stronger the prejudice becomes. Colossal harm and excessive violence might occur when illusions are challenged by external events. The challenges may be met with aggression and attempts at annihilation through fierce and violent supremacy. If this cannot be achieved, a far-reaching collapse of psychological and physical health in the narcissistic individual becomes likely. The absolute emotional need to continue to maintain this denial and avoidance explains the tenacity of such illusions, and the violence with which they will be defended. Although we have seen that environmental inadequacy is the crucial determining factor in the development of narcissism, it is not enough simply for the adult to shift environment as a means of changing personality. Indeed, it is more likely that the narcissistic person will attempt to violently change the environment and attempt to eliminate the challenge to their story. History is full of stories of despots and tyrants who attempt to change the world to fit in with the personal myth they need to tell about themselves. Characteristically, such individuals resort to more and more extreme behaviour as the story they have told themselves can no longer be sustained in the face of reality. History shows that despotism generally collapses as the selfhood of the despot fragments and collapses under the force of external challenges that make the illusion unsustainable. Small comfort oftentimes, as devastating harm is often done in the meantime.

As with all neurotic positions, the suffering narcissist will continue to behave as if the threat to self is still there, even though they may have grown up and the problematic childhood situation is long gone. It is important to realise that the narcissistic stance is not only a defence, it is also a lens through which the person views the world and for the narcissist, the world is a frightening, cold and dangerous place. Once again, like Narcissus, and because of emotional necessity the person misidentifies illusion with reality and where illusion and reality might contradict, the narcissist will always have to choose illusion. The true tragedy of the narcissistic state is here revealed in that what was first designed as a defence against an unbearable environment continues to resist all attempts at modification by the environment, even if the environment changes. The narcissistic state is a locked-in state and interprets all and every situation from the viewpoint of its own self-referencing needs. As is true in all emotional distortion and neurotic response, the personality continues to behave as if the environment is as it feels internally. The world feels threatening, therefore it is. This is especially true of very entrenched narcissistic states.

It is simply too much of an emotional risk to do any other than see monsters everywhere as, paradoxically, it is the continued presence of monsters that keeps us safe. If, for example, in order to protect ourselves from abandonment and disappointment we approach all relationships as if the person will eventually leave and disappoint us, we are safe. Alternatively, if we approach all relationships in a spirit of paranoia[13], expecting to be used or abused in some way, then likewise, we are safe. It is fairly predictable in each case that the feared thing will indeed happen only because we continually behave as if it will happen. In each case loyalty to the story, that might say something like 'people are either a let-down or abusers', protects us from vulnerability and the emotional pain of it happening. There is something of a pyrrhic victory over humiliation and torment if we can predict what is going to happen and if it means we are correct, once again, in our view of the world. If you are not a monster then we might want to come out of our hiding place and this is just too terrifying to contemplate. Therefore, a monster you will be and the whole edifice and distorted filter of the narcissistic stance is designed to prevent us from seeing anything else.

In the suffering adult the essential need to defend the self against emotional distress has coalesced and solidified into permanent distortions, leading to an impenetrable characterological change. Given the absolute emotional need to be safe and not to return to feelings of chaos or torment, the narcissistic adult possess powerful psychological predispositions to feel and behave as if the war is still raging, even though peace may have long been declared.

The narcissistic adult will therefore be subject to chronic, inflexible and disabling patterns of thought, feeling and behaviour reflecting their abusive or neglectful early environment. Patterns that will be wholly resistant to rational intervention. Such a person will operate from the undeveloped primary narcissistic position and be grandiose and exaggerate their achievements through storytelling, lying and deception. They will demand to be recognised in accordance with these qualities and as a superior person, without the need for objective verification. Whilst such a person may also sometimes appear as defeated and self-hating they will spend an inordinate amount of time secretly building and maintaining fantasies of greatness that focus on unequalled power, sexual prowess, genius levels of intellect or whatever quality the story requires. The emotional need to create and protect these self-soothing stories and the amount of ingenuity that goes into them cannot be overstated. Many years ago, I knew one grief-stricken and very disabled woman whose secret grandiosity rested upon the fact that she could bear more misery and degradation than anyone else. As a result of her tormented childhood and literally, tortured adulthood she could find no other means of generating self-esteem, self-significance and specialness.

Narcissistically wounded people will often feel that their true associates and peers should be people of equal status and consequently will be disdainful of the ordinary world and conventional people. Fantasies of omnipotence and magical dynamics will feature largely in such fiction. They may be attracted to interests that encourage and support such fantasy for example, spiritual or occult questing, 'healing' the planet or parts of it, fundamentalism or indeed, psychotherapy. They will almost certainly engage in activities and interests wherein they will feel misunderstood and marginalised in some way. They will also require and constantly demand excessive levels of admiration, attention and affirmation or failing this, will wish to be feared or notorious on the principle that if you can't be famous, be infamous. A lack of recognition or notoriety will be rationalised by an arrogant distain for the lack of appreciation in people at not recognising a genius when they see one. Following this, they will feel an absolute entitlement to recognition, will expect special and priority treatment, rage when this is not forthcoming and demand immediate and full gratification of any needs they might express – and needs they don't express. The person caught in the narcissistic state will equate 'I want' or 'I need' with 'they should give me' and for them there is no intermediary questioning the absolute rightness of this. Such individuals are wholly lacking in empathy and they do not experience any other person as having a reality other than how their gratification might be affected by those others. Reflecting very early developmental stages, everything that exists, exists as part of them. There is no capacity for external relationship and no ability to recognise the needs or emotions of others. Envy and paranoid experience will be an ever present feature of their emotions and their everyday state will be one of profound isolation, abstract misery and, whether expressed or not, considerable and barely contained rage and hatred. Such is the internal world of the narcissistically wounded person and whilst they may not dare to always express themselves in this way, indeed they may present to the world as quite the opposite character, the grandiose illusion will endure as an antagonist to external reality and be an indispensable refuge in an utterly intolerable world.

One feature of narcissistic behaviour is an ability and willingness to resort to considerable degrees of violence in defence of this rigid, yet highly brittle state. Narcissistic rage, like narcissism itself occurs on a continuum from displays of characteristic distain and aloofness, through irritation and outbursts of temper to extreme acts of violence. It is triggered by threats, not to the self and self-esteem but to the stability and legitimacy of the narcissistic posture. By this I mean, those threats that might lead to the narcissistic posture being exposed as the illusion it is and thereby fragmented. The narcissistic posture is constructed of internal fantasy and illusion and is extremely vulnerable to damage by incursion of external reality. We have also seen the deeply rooted psychological and emotional necessities underlying the construction of these illusions. For the narcissistic person, threats to the narcissistic posture are extremely serious. Such threats will be met with force and violence as the alternative is a return to the emotional and psychological maelstrom of terror and annihilation that was the beginning of the story. Narcissistic rage can take many forms extending from simple functional blindness, ignoring the threat to active ruthless pursuit and violent attack. Its function is to annihilate the threat to the narcissistic posture and the unsurpassed, most complex, developed and prevalent form of narcissistic rage is the revenge scenario.

Here, at last I can reveal my objection to revenge as a remedy and effective balm for the hurt it seeks to redress. I have shown in earlier chapters that the revenge scenario has all the hallmarks of a manoeuvre focussed on the deeply rooted self-regard of the revenger. It is not concerned with justice or fairness but with self-significance and 'thinking well of ourselves' on the individual and social stage. The revenger sets out to make themselves feel better about themselves and not to right a wrong. Their prime objective is to repair or reinstate the previously fragile mirror that contains their indispensable image. Revenge does not defend the self, but the image of the self and in this the revenger makes the same fundamental mistake as Narcissus. The revenger mistakes the image of the self for the self and is therefore protecting something that only exists in their own mind. Successful revenge perpetuates the delusion that safety is to be had in storytelling and ignores the possibility of a deeper, more securely rooted and less vulnerable emotional security. Such a deeper and less vulnerable security is to be found through returning to the unfinished work of the narcissistic transition and contains within in it the possibility that the need for violent revenge will become redundant.

For the narcissistically oriented revenger the prospect of turning to the (previously defeated) self has no attraction as they firmly believe it entails only feelings of loss, humiliation and powerlessness. The lack of interest shown by the revenger in anything other than revenge is precisely what will be encountered in any psychotherapeutically informed approach to the problem. To forgo revenge as a response to hurt is a near impossible task in such a situation as it requires a degree of willingness to bear the unbearable and confront an unimaginable humility that the person simply does not have the emotional resources to do. I have included, in chapter 10, a short case study which might go some way to illustrating the enormous difficulties encountered and perhaps some of the means of approaching them.

To conclude this chapter, I want to re-state my proposal that revenge is a massive and tragic instrumental error. I propose this for the reason that revenge ultimately reveals itself as unsustainable and inadequate in what it actually sets out to do. It works only partly and in working, merely reconstitutes the very dynamics that make revenge, and the suffering it encompasses, more likely in the future. Revenge may well be viewed as morally, ethically and rationally questionable but, ultimately this is a point of view and not an instrumental objection. My objection to revenge is instrumental in that it does not work. It does not work because it does nothing to address the pre-existing and highly vulnerable psychological and emotional states that make us so very prone to initiating revenge in the first place. It does not work because it is aimed squarely at avoiding ordinary human emotional states that are at the core of what it is to be human in an unpredictable, capricious and often dangerous world. Most of all, it does not work because it is primarily concerned with re-establishing an immature narcissistic state. It does nothing to encourage or establish a state of mature wellbeing and self-esteem. The successful prosecution of revenge only serves to reinstate and reinforce the ascendency of the highly vulnerable and fragile sense of self that is balanced precariously on the shoulders of primary narcissism. Furthermore, the successful prosecution of revenge dangerously encourages fragile illusions of grandiosity and omnipotence upon which the whole unstable structure rests. Revenge is so ubiquitous, predictably incessant, pernicious and dangerous because it feels like it works, when in fact it does not. It feels like it works in the same way that the original creation of our personal myth as our balm to an unhappy childhood felt like it worked.

I am proposing that there is a strong correlation between degrees of narcissism and the degree to which hurt and offended people will resort to and rely on the revenge scenario. The more narcissistically wounded we are, the more likely we are to choose revenge as a remedy for hurt. My submission therefore is that the 'cure' for the tragedy that is revenge lies not in moral reasoning, forgiveness or more effective jurisprudence but in diminishing the hold which a disproportionate primary narcissism has on the individual personality and upon group culture.

CHAPTER NINE

A lazy kind of grieving

At the end of the previous chapter I set out a basic rationale for my approach to the psycho-dynamics of the revenge scenario. This included its function in respect of the human psyche and the reasons for its ultimate failure to secure a sustainable and secure sense of well-being. As a response to the feelings arising from harm done and as a remedy for the vulnerability to future harm, revenge is far from sufficient. Worse than this, the illusions re-established by the revenge scenario itself positively encourage continuance of the very human vulnerability that makes revenge so inevitable, familiar and seductive in the first place. In this present chapter I want to move once again into established psychotherapeutic territory and focus on the specific elements of emotional and psychological life that are rendered exceptionally vulnerable by an attachment to the narcissistic state. I will also show, in each case, how revenge fantasies and actions might serve to create the illusion of sanctuary in the face of such vulnerabilities.

Omnipotence[1] is characteristic of early life and most infants and children develop fantasies of unlimited power and magical abilities. In the young child, as it becomes aware of its dependency on an unreliable and capricious world, fantasies of omnipotence can help to reduce anxieties arising in response to threats involving abandonment, neglect and overwhelming feelings of helplessness. It can be the redeeming factor when potency is humbled by reality. In healthy development the support of a benign and loving carer will enable the infant to eventually forego omnipotence through accommodating ordinary dependency and relative feelings of helplessness and humility. In this way, the anxieties and dependencies are no longer felt to be life-threatening, but as unpleasant yet normal parts of any relationship. An image, an introject[2], of the benign care-giver may be incorporated into the psychological make-up of the child thus enabling the child to feel that such qualities belong to themselves and are within their sphere of control. In this way, introjection becomes one of the building blocks of future self-esteem and is an example of the reliance that the child has on their care givers for developing psychological health. Introjection of what was previously an external relationship enables the child to begin to treat itself in the way it has been treated; to self soothe in the way it has been soothed and to self-regard and self-love in the way it has been regarded and loved. Frustrations that were previously agonising and necessitated omnipotent fantasy to manage now belong to disturbing and painful, but bearable, experience and can be lived through without the need for distortions of reality. Such a fortunate child is likely to develop an adaptive and realistic sense of their own potency and will be able to face limitation and helplessness without excessive humiliation or self-fragmentation.

However, where the child has been less fortunate, and in the absence of the adaptive mechanisms provided by loving and helpful introjections, thoughts and acts of revenge can supply the vehicle to sustain, or re-animate, the necessary fantasies of omnipotence. The omnipotent fantasy is a core element of both the narcissistic state and the revenge scenario. It is one of the self-soothing mechanisms that bring comfort and refuge from an uncontrollable world that has so hurt and humiliated us. In this way the revenge scenario can be understood as arising in defence of the narcissistic state when the narcissistic state itself is threatened with fragmentation by a world that can no longer be sufficiently denied. Because they only aim to re-establish the pre-existing narcissistic state, thoughts and acts of revenge do not bring enduring and sustainable relief from hurt or anxieties about hurt. That the pre-existing narcissistic state is what causes the person to be so prone to revenge in the first place explains why such acts demonstrate an infinitely circular progression in human affairs. Revenge is a defence of a defence and does nothing to address the deeper underlying vulnerability.

I think the impulse to revenge and the narcissistic state are intimately related. There is a complementary economy between the two in that the greater the narcissism, the stronger will be the impulse to revenge and the more irresistible the urge to act on that impulse.

Furthermore, the two are related even more intimately in that the impulse to revenge will appropriate all the primitive elements of primary narcissism (fantasies of omnipotence and brilliance, entitlement and elite privilege, absence of empathy, ruthless and exploitative treatment of others, mendacity, arrogance and rage) and employ these to potentiate, legitimise and carry out any actions contemplated by the revenger. The most potent of these elements will coalesce around the various projections[3], introjections and associated identifications, such as idealisation and demonisation that inevitably form part of the revenge scenario.

'Projective identification', recognised and described by Melanie Klein[4] in 1946, was a significant development in the understanding of narcissism. Projective identification essentially describes a psychological process aimed at transferring unwanted feelings, or unacceptable parts of the self, to other people who are then seen to be the originators of such qualities. Projective identification is a term used to describe a psychological process whereby parts of the self are forced into another person who then becomes identified with whatever has been projected. The person doing the projecting strives to find the projected qualities in the other person and, additionally, will induce them to behave as if they are the very embodiment of the projection. Projective identification differs from simple projection in that projective identification influences the projectee to behave as if the projection did indeed belong to them. The second person is provoked by the projection and begins to behave as though he or she is in fact actually characterised by the projected behaviours, thoughts or attitudes. This process commonly happens unconsciously and outside the awareness of both parties involved. Reconsidering the earlier example wherein the story we tell ourselves is that 'everyone lets me down eventually' it will be found that the mechanisms of projective identification operate to incite people to behave in just such a way. This is a subtle process, to the point of being unconscious and often undetectable in the relationship but, nevertheless, it will commonly be found such a relationship does indeed end in disappointment and feelings of betrayal. In this way, projective identification also contributes to the repetition compulsion[5] and in this respect may help to understand the 'logic' of this apparently self-defeating behaviour.

Projective identification forms the underpinnings of the basic psychological manoeuvre that manifests as prejudice and scapegoating.

Projection of bad feelings, and bad parts of the self, is a means of coping with self-persecutory anxiety and the self-hatred that will arise if the person views the self as impotent or 'hateful' in some other way. The narcissistically fragile person cannot bear self-hurts or self-insults as they threaten to reveal a terrifyingly vulnerable inadequacy. Thus, we can say that one function of the revenge scenario is to transfer self-hatred, and violence to the self, to someone else. The psychoanalyst and criminologist, Arthur Hyatt-Williams[6] identified these projective mechanisms operating in conditions of latent murderousness and recognised that the hateful or murderous acts can be interpreted as projecting an unbearable state of mind into another person, thereby gaining some relief. He wrote of one of his clients: 'projective identification, in which the projectee experiences what has been put into him…[the revenger] is then freed from an unbearable state of mind. It can be and often is reversed, so that what is put into someone is returned. This is what he [the revenger] seemed to do, returning much of his own violence in the process[7]'. In other words, by forcing the other person to feel the way we have been made to feel, we get some relief from those feelings in that they have been given to someone else. Relief is also gained from the fact that, in imagination, the other person now carries the guilt and remorse and obligations for reparation. Moreover, Hyatt-Williams demonstrated that when projective identification becomes revengeful, violent murderousness will operate at great distances in time and place from the original insult and substitute victims will serve just as well as the 'real' offender.

During the late 1950's, developments in the theory of projective identification proposed that it had two functions and, like narcissism, healthy and unhealthy variants. Firstly, and benignly, projective identification might be employed to interject a state of mind into another person in order to communicate with them about that state. For example, a crying baby will communicate its distress clearly by interjecting that state into the mother. A more sophisticated example would be that of passive aggression. Though not overtly hostile, passive aggression will generate a feeling of hostility in the recipient, thereby accurately communicating the emotional state of the passive aggressor. In this way a person can let someone else know that they are angry, not by expressing their anger, but by making the other person feel angry. This form of communication is very common in everyday life and can be employed to try and communicate every type of feeling, not just anger. Unfortunately, as a means of communication it is tortuously indirect and highly ineffective. However, the phenomenon is well understood in psychotherapeutic theory and the psychotherapist will have learned to examine their own feelings for information about what a client might be feeling. Additionally, the client may gain a degree of vicarious relief by witnessing their own feelings, which might be impossible or dangerous to express directly, expressed by another person.

The second function of projective identification has already been described and is the evacuation of an unbearable state of mind and forcing that state into another. In this we discover the truest reason for the prosecution of the revenge scenario as might ever be described. The psychoanalyst, Wilfred Bion[8] described abnormal projective identification as a 'violent evacuation[9]' and it is precisely this that the revenger wishes to achieve. Specifically, revengeful thoughts and actions are a violent evacuation of defeat, humiliation, shame and grief. This is achieved through by violently paying back to the wrongdoer the unendurable feeling state the revenger.

In summary, normal and healthy projective identification can be distinguished from the abnormal and unhealthy by the extent of the violence and the degree of omnipotence involved. Unhealthy projective identification will also be characterised by the degree to which the intention is to support the re-constitution of a fragmented narcissistic state. Therefore, in respect of the projective function of the impulse to revenge I am proposing that, in seeking to defend against threats to a fragile narcissistic equilibrium (arising from external reality and especially events that challenge primitive narcissistic illusions of omnipotence) the revenge response misappropriates all the power and mechanisms of the narcissistic state and attempts to evacuate back into the world all the unbearable states of mind that would otherwise remain with the revenger. Furthermore, from the 'communicative' perspective the revenger seeks to stimulate sympathy and understanding and even to enlist support in their venture. To the extent that revenge is taken, and seen to be taken, we are also communicating just how wronged we have been and how right we are to act in this way.

In the last years of the sixteenth century, a whole genre of dramatic works appeared, known collectively as the Revenge

Tragedies. The best known of these is Shakespeare's Hamlet and in the closing moments of the play, Horatio reveals the essential truth of the purposes and psychological flaws contained in the revenge scenario just witnessed by the audience.

> '...so shall you hear
> Of carnal, boldly, and unnatural acts,
> Of accidental judgements, casual slaughters,
> Of deaths put upon by cunning and forced cause,
> And, in all this upshot, purposes mistook
> Fall'n on the inventor heads.[10]'

Shakespeare himself, and the Elizabethan and Jacobean audience, appeared to be all too aware of the 'purposes mistook' of the revenge scenario. The revenge tragedies: the poisoned picture of The White Devil (Webster, 1612), the poisoned skull of The Revenger's Tragedy (Tourneur, 1606) and the love potion of The Changeling (Middleton, Rowley, 1653) reveal an enduring attachment and fascination with the drama of the unfolding impulse to revenge. Such drama begins with the Greek tragedies and emerges intact, and plainly recognisable in its legacy, in the cinema of the present day. I would suggest that the fascination lies partly in the intrigue, mastery of deception, treachery, mendacity, black humour and overt violence but also in the fact that the audience knows, without doubt, that the protagonists are making painfully familiar and transparently obvious psychological mistakes. The audience also know that there will not be a happy ending. There is a degree of vicarious relief in witnessing such drama, together with recognition of an all too human predicament. We return home with a sense of 'there but for the grace of god' and glad that, this time, it was not us. We may also, as civilised people, like to congratulate ourselves at being above such primitive meanderings. In my terms, the foundation of these 'mistakes' is the degree to which the processes of projective identification are employed, together with the necessary distortions of reality that will inevitably follow. Excessive and abnormal projective identification is the core tool of the trade of the revenger and the means by which they both undertake and justify their actions. Little surprise to find that projective identification is the essential psychological dramatic manoeuvring for the protagonists in the revenge tragedy.

Before I can leave this exploration of the interplay between narcissism and projective identification I want to draw out another of the elements found in the revenge drama. True to the eternal circumlocutions of the revenge drama, the revenger will both be aroused by envy and will misappropriate the psychological mechanisms of envy to prosecute and justify their actions. Envy is a crucial part of the revenge drama but, before exploring this in more detail, it might help to clarify some of the ideas relating to envy if I first write a short account of what psychotherapists mean when they talk about 'good' and 'bad' objects.

Psychoanalyst, Melanie Klein[4] developed a view of narcissism that focussed on the central role of fantasy and storytelling and relied heavily upon a defensive manoeuvre she called 'splitting'. In this, the infant or young child will manage distressing and ambivalent experiences in life by creating a view of people and objects in the world not as a realistic mixtures of good and bad qualities, sometimes gratifying and at other times frustrating, but rather each person or object becomes designated by the child as wholly 'good' or wholly 'bad'. Klein proposed that this psychological splitting manoeuvre was central to narcissism and would be carried over into adulthood in cases of unmodified narcissism. Thus, at immature stages of development a caregiver, or other person in the infant's life, can only be 'all good' or 'all bad' and not a mixture of both. This (healthy) splitting of good from bad helps the struggling, helpless and dependent child cope with what would otherwise be terrible anxiety at realising that the world is a capricious and unpredictable place over which they have no reliable control. That the world might contain people who are both *good and bad* is too psychologically complex for the infant mind to process. The maturing child, with the support of a loving and empathetic care giver, may learn to cope with this realisation and begin to tolerate ambivalence and frustration and hence begin to forego the need for a splitting manoeuvre. Relationships may become 'whole' again with each person, including the self, being a source of both satisfaction and frustration, of fulfilment and disappointment. This leads to the possibility of more realistic and mature relationships. The adult who has successfully enough negotiated the path away from primitive, splitting narcissism will take the good with the bad whereas, the adult who has failed in this will split the good from the bad. Never the twain shall meet, except in enmity and violence.

In primitive narcissism, the infant feels themselves to be the source of all goodness and satisfaction and the discovery that this is not the case gives rise to hatred. Envy can be described as a form of hatred and a desire to hurt, or spoil, the source of life and goodness following a realisation that this source lies outside of the self and is therefore beyond control. In the adult, the expression of envy is always characterised as a desire to spoil the 'good' object. In this it might be distinguished from jealousy, which is a desire to possess the good object. Envy is therefore far more primitive, belonging to the realm of unmodified narcissism, and presents a terrible dilemma for the infant (and consequently the adult) who find themselves subject to both desire and hatred towards the same object. A familiar element in the revenge scenario is the splitting of 'good' and 'bad' and the desperate attempt to disallow an amalgam of the two in the same place. Indeed, Kleinian 'splitting' and following this, poor discrimination between the good and the bad is one the core failings, the 'purposes mistook', of the theatrical tragedy of the revenge drama.

Lying at the heart of this need to keep good and bad separate is an immature and illusory wish to protect the 'good' from what might otherwise be an envious attack. If a person is at different times good and bad, frustrating and gratifying, it becomes extremely problematic for the young child (and narcissistically primitive adult) to reconcile these contradictory feelings. During psychotherapeutic work, the familiar insistence of the client on, for example, 'mother-good/father-bad', or 'him-good/her-bad', or vice versa, or any of a multitude of variants, is an obstacle to progressing towards abating the destructive consequences of the unmodified narcissistic state.

At first glance, the role played by envy in revenge may not be immediately clear as the offender is the 'bad' object and therefore will not stimulate an envious attack. However, if we consider more closely the role of the narcissistic state in the drama, it is possible to see how the offender becomes the 'good' object. From the perspective of the revenger, the offender is the 'good' object as it is they who are triumphant and who have possession of the good feeling. The revenger, as a result of their unmodified narcissism, feels their (narcissistic) stability to be exceptionally threatened by witnessing the offender get away with the good feelings. Unbearably for the revenger, the offender has taken possession of the good feelings and is now 'getting away' with them. The revenger, through the misappropriation of all the power and aggression of envious mechanisms, will evacuate their 'badness' (impotence, humiliation, loss), force it into the offender and thereby spoil the 'good' in the offender. In the most brutal and violent way, this is what the rapist does.

In addition to envy, the revenger will commonly be subject to strong paranoid fantasies. The envious forcing of the unbearable state of the revenger into the offender in order to occupy and spoil their good state will produce equally violent fantasies of retaliation. This will particularly be the case where the revenger's hold on omnipotent fantasy is fragmenting. The 'intact' narcissist feel themselves to be invincible whereas the 'wounded' narcissist does not. Indeed, this awareness of danger may further reinforce the need for re-doubled fantasies of omnipotence or intensified and unassailable violence in the first strike of the revenge drama. We commonly see in the theatrical revenge drama, as the body count rises, the impulses are not moderated but amplified. Such is the greed of the revenger and a further indication that revenge is indeed founded upon 'purposes mistook'. The escalation reflects an attempt to restore the narcissistic state. The 'mistake' arising because restoration will not be, through revenge, achieved in any reliable way that will diminish further impulses to revenge.

As with the blood feud, the mechanisms of revenge and attempts at narcissistic re-stabilisation offer no possibility of an anxiety free, sustainable and stable psychological resolution. However, it may be that not all actors in the drama carry such narcissistic fragility and the possibility emerges of addressing the narcissistic wound itself in a quest for a sustainable resolution. Of this, more later, but for now a clue suggesting a different kind of resolution lies at the dénouement of another of Shakespeare's tragedies suggesting contemplations on immense grief and mourning:

'A glooming peace this morning with it brings:
The sun for sorrow will not show its head.
Go hence to have more talk of these sad things.
Some shall be pardon'd, and some punishéd,
For never was a story of more woe
Than this of Juliet and her Romeo[11]'.

At this point, I want to return to the beginning and remind ourselves of two of the most essential and basic of all emotional defences: denial and distraction. In everyday life there are many occasions when our emotional experience is such that denial and distraction becomes, if not absolutely necessary, then highly desirable. There are many ways in which the emotional and psychological mechanisms of revenge can be successfully employed to help in coping with routine and distressing emotional states. In conjunction with this, I want to begin to introduce yet another aspect of the revenge scenario: the role plays in the dynamics of human relationships. The revengeful relationship is a singularly intense, intimate and tenaciously attached bond. It is perhaps no surprise that love and marriage, when turned to the shadows can support a pitiless degree of revengeful experience that can endure, seemingly without end. The American psychoanalyst, Lucy LaFarge reminds us, 'one does not fall out of hate as readily as one falls out of love'[12]. The revengeful relationship tends strongly towards the obsessional. The revenger, in ways that hold complete dominion over their conscious and unconscious selves, urgently tries to exploit the target of their obsession and triumph over a desperately painful state of mind.

The first of these routinely practiced, day-to-day uses of revenge is to provide a defence (denial and distraction) against feelings of impotence and consequent shame or humiliation. As a defence against unbearable states of mind, omnipotence has already been described. Shame might be defined as an experience of seeing ourselves in the absence of any points of reference which provide affirmation of ourselves as 'good'. On our own terms, and with reference to our personal values and beliefs, we see ourselves as deficient, as 'bad' and are thereby ashamed. Humiliation is an associated emotion, to which we are particularly vulnerable, and can be defined as an experience of our shame being witnessed by non-empathetic other people. To maintain an image of the self as adequately potent is an essential ingredient in our protection against existential vulnerability, maintaining adequate self-regard and thus avoiding feelings of shame and humiliation. How each of us defines 'adequate potency' will be a direct reflection of our degree of narcissism and consequent need for relative dominion. For example, the extreme narcissist may define 'adequate' as nothing less than domination of the entire world. For the narcissistically challenged adult, the experience of being harmed by others, and being witnessed in this harm, is deeply corrosive to an already fragile self-esteem. Thoughts and acts of revenge, real or imagined, can offer the promise of reconstitution in such a case. Shame, and particularly if it develops to humiliation through being witnessed by others, is deeply corrosive and might be made even more so by the addition of further shame fantasies of paranoia flavour. Paranoid shame stems from the feeling that humiliation is deliberately engineered by others or, from the belief that humiliation is a sign of utter rejection and social annihilation leading to unbearable experiences of desolation. In the case of imagining a deliberately humiliating hurt, the situation will inevitably give rise to paranoid shame and following this, the propensity towards revenge is colossal. Revenge promises that the offender will feel the shame that the revenger is currently feeling. In addition, shame fantasies may begin to imagine that the humiliation and impotence can be redeemed by returning it to the imagined source (paying back) and, buoyed by grandiose righteousness, such a return can rightfully be carried out with impunity and without consequence. In this respect, the function of revenge might be further summarised in realising that by focussing on a righteous and wholly justified claim to a fully warranted retribution, the revenger entitles themselves to discharge all the power of pitiless violence and envious aggression, prove their potency, nullify their humiliation and do that which is right and good. The revenger begins their journey as an impotent villain and ends it a hero.

We have seen that revenge is very commonly fuelled by narcissistic rage and is a violent attempt to restore the grandiose self. Such rage is triggered by a threat or injury to the idealised, imaginary self. The unendurable feelings of vulnerability, impotence and humiliation will seek to restore themselves through violence. The revenge drama, and the focus on that particular 'someone' who's done something wrong provides a very primitive attempt to restore the grandiose and omnipotent self by giving structure and direction to an otherwise amorphous and chaotic rage. This is the key to understanding the crucial importance of identifying the wrong and the wrongdoer. In the absence of such an external focus we will be chaotically flailing in a blind, impotent rage, which threatens to immolate the self. A focussed and targeted hatred is exceedingly stabilising to an unstable and fragmenting personality. In employing the entire armoury provided by the mechanisms of primitive narcissism, the revenger transforms the offender into a monstrous nemesis and reduces them to a monolithic structure of one terrible event, one unredeemable character trait and one unendurable grievance. The revenger becomes for ever affirmed as a 'good' person, wholly justified and righteous, and will be utterly purged of any previous humiliation or impotence through what they are about to do.

There is a compelling development here when we link the wish for revenge to the need to maintain a positive sense of individual meaning and narrative. If humiliation is a result of shame being witnessed by others, it may only be fully redeemed if the successful act of revenge is likewise witnessed, and this time applauded, thereby enhancing the value to the revengers' social value. We might recall Eliot's prompting that human beings are all 'absorbed in an endless struggle to think well of themselves'. From this perspective, the hurt that kindles the wish for revenge is felt by the revenger to have a destructive impact on his sense of individual meaning and self-importance in the eyes of others. The 'audience', by witnessing the humiliation, increases the potential for a vastly amplified humiliation. The revenger's concern now becomes to redeem not only their narrative importance internally but also in the imagined and real eyes of those others to whom this recognition and validation is of critical significance. The injury thus becomes a meaning-disrupting injury and leads to a struggle to re-establish an adequate sense of self in the eyes of the (imagined) audience to the revenger's narrative. Once again, what defines 'adequate' will be influenced by relative degrees of narcissism present. The role of storytelling in the maintenance of the narcissistic self thus takes on a new dimension and includes the imaginer and their audience, the protagonist and the admiring, adoring or disapproving and vilifying onlookers.

The wish for revenge, together with the desire to be seen by others to be taking rightful revenge, is central to retaining these illusions as intact and stable. We can see that using the revenge scenario to restore a damaged sense of individual meaning and value, and to make this known to others, is a central and recurring theme in the revenge tragedy. For example, throughout Tourneur's 'Revenge Tragedy' (1606) the revenger, the appropriately named Vindice, maintains a running monologue of asides directed to the audience, justifying his actions and seeking approval, revelling in his brilliance at deception and successfully carrying out his plans. In Shakespeare's Othello[13] we see Iago doing very much the same. They are acting as much to reclaim the admiration of the audience as for themselves.

The second, commonplace, denial and distraction function of revenge is that it can provide a reliable promise of comfort and refuge from emotional torment in a way that other addictive behaviours will. Revenge can be something reliable, readily available and accessible. It is the habitual revenger's drug of choice. As an addictive device, revenge has the central defining characteristics common to all addictions: that it promises to deliver, provides a believable illusion of delivery, but is ultimately unsatisfying and leaves us wanting more. All addictive behaviours, revenge being no exception, are an almost achieved attempt to ward off unbearable feelings and states of mind through attempting to control and regulate the person's emotional state. It is correct to call the revengeful relationship an addictive relationship in that it is founded upon the same obsessional ideation and compulsive enactment that characterises all addictions. Psychotherapeutic theory refers to addictions as 'narcissistic behaviour disorders' and proposes that the drug, or compulsive behaviour, is not a substitute for lost or absent loving persons, or for a relationship with them, but is a replacement for the narcissistic chasm that exists in the person's personality. This is a direct echo of my earlier assertion that revenge doesn't work. It doesn't work for the same reason that addictions do not work. Addictive substances are not a substitute for something good or nourishing; rather they are an attempt to reconstitute the primitive narcissistic state. This state can only be shored up at great cost and will inevitably remain highly unstable and for ever vulnerable.

Addictive behaviour (and revenge) is a response to a collapse of omnipotence and the gross imaginary overvaluation of the self. Overvaluation is necessary to maintain stability of the narcissistic state. Disintegration occurs following an abysmal disappointment and humiliation when these illusions are inevitably shattered by life experience. It is this appalling and unbearable disappointment and humiliation that leads to the addictive quest and, I might add, to the revenge quest. The shattered illusions generate a narcissistic crisis of catastrophic proportions as external reality forces the devastating realisation that the person is not in control of the core of themselves. The addicts' essential but illusory sense of mastery and self-esteem threatens to collapse in on itself in the face of reality and, in their desperation, they refuse to admit that they are not in control. This is the very core of the personal emotional crisis that generates both addiction and the impulse to revenge. The drive to addiction, like the impulse to revenge, is in the service of narcissistic equilibrium and not of movements towards psychological and emotional maturity and health. Both addictive behaviour and revengeful behaviour are desperate attempts to re-establish lost and disintegrating illusions of internal stability and external potency. The desperation and violence with which both the addict and the revenger will pursue their aim constitutes raging and defiant determination to preserve at any cost their illusory stability. Furthermore, in their grandiosity, the addict/revenger will absolutely believe that they are entitled to act in this way. Violence will erupt consequent upon undeniable rights to destroy or exploit anyone who challenges this. Revealing the same parentage of the addict and the revenger, Heinz Kohut[14] wrote that the motive force in both behaviours is narcissistic rage. Narcissistic rage, he pointed out is characterised by its deeply anchored unrelenting compulsion, its utter disregard for reasonable limitations and its boundlessness. Revenge is an addictive phenomenon and both addiction and revenge do not work in a sustainable and reliable way. They are both tragically flawed in being geared to re-establishing only the unstable and fragile narcissism and not at constituting a mature, constant and reality-based self-esteem.

The third day-to-day way in which the revenge drama might be employed is in recognising its inherent capacity to create intimacy and an enduring relationship with another person. That such a negatively oriented impulse might be seen is this way may appear strange but the relationship between the revenger and their victim is as tenacious as it is intimate. It can be an aberrant but effective balm for deepest feelings of loneliness and abandonment. Hollywood movie makers have long used this characteristic of the revenge scenario to portray some disturbing stories. A number of films immediately spring to mind where the profound solitude and isolation of the revenger is soothed by an enduring and obsessional relationship with the victim: Fatal

Attraction (1987), Sleeping with the Enemy (1991) and The Hand that Rocks the Cradle (1992)[15] are three such films. The revengeful relationship might be felt by the revenger to lessen the distress of isolation and meaninglessness.

The term 'attachment disorder[16]' was fashioned to describe a group of human emotional problems that have a characteristically disruptive impact on relationships with others. In brief, attachment disorder refers to a persistent personal preference for making adult relationships in a way that seeks to remedy frustrations and traumas left over from childhood experience. 'He's looking for a mother figure' or 'she's looking for a father figure' would be common, everyday expressions that might point to the existence of an attachment disorder. By re-enacting in adulthood something that resembles the childhood relationship, the adult may be attempting to reconcile some unfinished emotional business from a frustrating or traumatic childhood. This type of repetition compulsion illustrates the common tendency to repeat into adulthood near identical traumatic or unsatisfactory childhood relationships, in the hope of a different outcome. Repetition is an attempt at mastery of something that has previously defeated us. 'Disorder' is a strong term as every adult relationship contains some demands and elements that stem from frustrated childhood wishes. We might be more concerned however, if a person shows repeated, forceful and futile attempts to re-enact elements of their childhood in adult relationships, in the hope of reconciling childhood distress. For example, abandonment and powerlessness as a child might manifest itself as an adult relationship style centred on high demands for constant contact, jealousy or paranoia and controlling and manipulative behaviour. Alternatively, sexual exploitation in childhood may result in adult relationships that are characterised by extreme ambivalence and confusions about sexuality, sexual behaviour, sensuality and non-sexual rapport. Confusion between the demands of un-met childhood needs and what might reasonably be expected in an adult relationship is a common cause of relationship distress and breakdown. Furthermore, where un-met childhood needs overlap with narcissistic tendencies, the potential for major conflict and hurt is increased. It is highly probable in such an instance that either, or both, of the frustrated and disappointed couple may resort to prolonged and ferocious revenge tactics to assuage age-old feelings of disappointment, re-enacted powerlessness, humiliation and loss. For example, in marital states it might be that the husband receives raging and vengeful demands that more correctly belong with the wife's father, and vice versa with respect to the husband's mother.

The relationship between revenger and revenge is as intimate, powerful and tenacious as any we might imagine. I have already described its quality as addictive in that the relationship forever holds the false promise of satisfaction for the revenger. The revengeful relationship itself might easily become a symbol for all the hope of redemption, the promise, that is ever present in the 'almost had' nature of the narcissistic experience. To give up the revengeful relationship would be to give up hope of personal redemption. Additionally, the revengeful relationship offers some possibility of continuing to avoid the essential ambivalence inevitably accompanying any relationship. The revenger, at all costs, wishes to avoid ambivalence. Unfortunately for the revenger, sustainable resolution and emotional maturity involves embracing ambivalence and not in avoiding it.

In this respect, the revengeful relationship can be seen to perpetuate the dilemma, to keep alive the possibility of resolution, by creating an enduring relationship to what the Scottish psychoanalyst, Ronald Fairbairn[17] called the 'exciting/rejecting' object or the 'alluring' object. Fairbairn recognised that the object (person) who provides life sustaining gratification must also inevitably provide endless frustration. For the infant, the caregiver at once becomes infinitely desirable and infinitely hateful. We have seen that the resolution of this dilemma, of coming to terms with the limitations of love, rage, despair, comfort, hope, gratification, betrayals and abandonment, is a core requirement of emotional maturity and a development away from primitive narcissism. The revenge drama, and the relationships it creates, is a representation of an enduring connection to this exciting/rejecting person. As with the addiction scenario, the degree to which the revengeful relationship endures will be the degree to which the revenger maintains the violent, though forlorn, hope of a non-ambiguous outcome.

Attachment theory[18] and psychoanalytic theory have common roots but have evolved differently. Attachment theorists would propose that their work is a reaction against and a corrective to, the solipsistic core of the classical psychoanalytic stance. The main divergence is the relative emphasis that is placed on internal, purely psychological experience (psychoanalytic) versus external, real experience as mediated by a relationship with people (attachment theory). However, convergence emerges in that both schools highlight a concern with the significance of subjective experience in infancy and, to use attachment terminology, 'felt security'. To use our earlier example of a child who experiences sexual exploitation: this may result in difficulties in integrating specifically sexual feeling with general attachment feeling and can manifest itself in adult relational styles that are simultaneously overly sexualised and avoidant or extremely ambivalent. Disorganised, split-ambivalent and disorientated attachment behaviour in adulthood is strongly associated with the narcissistic state and is one of the behavioural consequences. Such behaviour is strongly associated with childhood experiences of abandonment and maltreatment and is highly predictive of the kind of violence in adults that instils a preference for the revengeful relationship. Such violence will have underpinnings of injustice and insult, outrage, the imperative to pursue and punish the offender, together with pride and righteousness in the pursuit, and a relief in the successful execution of the task. The revenger, through the relentless and intimate pursuit of this particular style of relationship with their victim, is thereby pursuing the hope of resolution of failures that occurred in consequence of their earlier child-parent relationship style. That the original trauma, or insult, may be located at a time and place many years in the past and the offending people no longer available does not prevent revenge processes occurring here and now and with whoever is close at hand.

Finally in this chapter, it has been observed that revenge is a 'lazy form of grief' and amongst the many clichés about revenge, it is one of the best. Any kind of hurt received involves losses and part of recovering from such a hurt will mean accommodating and mourning these losses. Loss of feelings of invincibility and safety, loss of power in not being able to stop the hurt, loss of face at the same thing, loss of faith in humanity or the standard of fairness and perhaps most of all, loss of the love and regard that we had wished for. A revengeful response can be a way of arresting the emotional consequences of these losses by raging against the reality of them. At the very least, the revenge quest can assist in creating a compelling and seductive fantasy that such losses are only temporary and all can be regained.

Throughout this book I have moved in one direction to assert progressively that the impulse to revenge arises out of, and is constructed from elements of, a primitive narcissistic state. It must therefore follow that any resolution of the impulse must proceed through a resolution of that narcissistic state. I have focussed in some detail on the aetiology and dynamics of the narcissistic state but to simplify once again: the primitive narcissistic state persists when the infant is unable to mourn the loss of omnipotence and all it signifies. These losses inevitably occur when infant development towards a healthy, self-conscious adult state encounters the capricious and, sometimes disappointing and hurtful, external world. The revenger is one who has no resources enabling them to bear such losses.

To anticipate the next chapter, it follows from this that any psychotherapeutic process that attempts to address the primary narcissism/revenge correlation must have, at its very heart, a process of mourning. Revenge is an attempt to protect the narcissistic state from fragmentation; the narcissistic state is a defence against mourning, therefore, revenge is protection from the pain of unbearable and irreconcilable mourning. In the next chapter I want to present a fictional case study and I am hopeful that this will demonstrate my proposals and illustrate possibilities for resolution. Additionally, I will present a method of working psychotherapeutically that tried to usefully modify persistent and ingrained impulses to revenge in one individual, thereby reducing the life-long suffering and isolation he experienced.

CHAPTER TEN

Turn your grievance into grieving...

Working as a psychotherapist with clients who present substantial and entrenched propensities to revengeful thought and action, either in fantasy or in reality, presents one of the most difficult challenges I encounter. The process is nothing less than trying to support the client in bearing the unbearable. In the chronically entrenched revengeful person, the combination of narcissistic imperative and habitual discharge through revenge fantasy will make a positive therapeutic outcome difficult, if not impossible. However, my experience is also that revengeful processes operate to some degree in the majority of clients and I have found less entrenched dynamics are amenable to therapeutic intervention and result in positive outcomes. I think that shifting the psychotherapeutic focus onto the narcissistic intra-psychic component of revengeful behaviour, rather than a focus on moral or cognitive reasoning, has proved helpful in arresting this most destructive of human cyclical behaviours. I have witnessed many positive outcomes using this approach with clients who had initially presented with very long-standing and seemingly intractable difficulties.

My interest in the matter began some time ago during encounters with my own impulses to revenge when I was working with groups and individuals, post-civil war, in an ex-Yugoslav country. In my work, I came across stories and heard about experiences involving resolute desires for revenge that appeared to defeat all attempts at intervention, let alone resolution. After being immersed in this for some time, and doing my best with the stories I was hearing, a startling thing began to happen. As part of my own emotional responses I began to be aware of impulses to revenge myself on these people, in particular by abandoning them and humiliating them in some undefined way. On reflection, I was aware of a growing anger in myself, which I imagined expressing by refusing to visit and work there anymore. I was curious about this response and, allowing the fantasy to unfold in my mind, I discovered a personal revenge scenario developing. I imagined telling the groups that their problems were just too extreme for anyone to deal with; they were unredeemable and far too primitive and resistant to change for me to waste my time there anymore. Omnipotent revenge indeed.

As we saw in the previous chapter, through the mechanisms of projective identification it is usual for a psychotherapist to begin to experience the feelings contained in the stories they might be working with. Feelings will be experienced as if they were their own feelings and, from a technical perspective, can give the therapist useful information about the client's feeling state. This probably explains some of what was happening to me in that I was receiving information about the latent desires for revenge in the people I was working with. However, I felt that this was not a complete and satisfying explanation. Something else was happening in that I was also aware of feeling insulted by them. I was feeling humiliated and diminished as a potent therapist. This was wholly irrational but, nevertheless, there it was. I, in turn, began to feel an irrational impulse to pay them back insult for insult, like for like. In my distress, I wanted them to feel bad in the way that I sometimes felt bad when working with them. I was feeling unskilled, useless and humiliated.

20 years later, I am still working in the area and my understanding, uncomfortable though it was to discover both intellectually and emotionally, was that my apparent inability to help resolve the difficulties was challenging my own grandiosity and, at times, my self-identity as a competent psychotherapist. My fantasy of omnipotence as a psychotherapist, my narcissistic need to be potent in the group, was being frustrated by the astonishing obstinacy of the difficulties we were all facing. I was struggling to manage the limitations of my professional potency and translating this into feelings of personal humiliation and loss of esteem. Being defeated in a professional situation I so much wished to be master of, my own impulses to revenge were triggered as a defence against my own narcissistic annihilation. I was a long way from home and working alone but I do remember a close friend at the time prompting me to

recall the real difficulties of the task I grandly imagined I could achieve and counselling me simply to 'grow up and join the ordinary human race'. The ensuing grief and humbling realisation of the death of my fantasy was painful but not, I discovered, wholly annihilating. Over time my humiliation, and my painful acceptance of it, enabled us all to progress with an increasingly realistic agenda. An agenda involving less anxiety and violence and characterised a mutual compassionate understanding of the limitations of psychotherapy and of humanity. Paradoxically, it was apparent that this was precisely the emotional and psychological work the group's themselves were struggling so hard with. Struggles that had for so long resulted in intractable impulses to revenge and the subsequent inevitable misery.

How, then, does someone so attached to fantasy, so in need of grandiose omnipotent self-regard, that without it believe they will fragment and disappear in chaos and terminal rage, ever begin to 'grow up and join the ordinary human race?' To start to answer this question I want to return briefly to some aspects of relevant psychotherapeutic theory and then try to demonstrate how this might look in clinical practice. In the previous chapter, I introduced the idea that very young infants will tend to split persons and objects into clear black or white categories, 'good' or 'bad'. I suggested that such splitting is done in an attempt to control chaotic and disturbing feelings that may ensue if a more realistic ambivalence was allowed. These ideas first emerged in the pre and post WWII era through the writings of Melanie Klein[1], and were subsequently developed by psychoanalysts Wilfred Bion[2] and Hannah Segal[3] and through the British analysts Ronald Fairbairn[4] and Donald Winnicot[5]. Collectively, the body of thought became known as Object Relations theory. Object Relations theory has been immensely influential on contemporary psychotherapeutic practice. I think it is helpful to articulate the basis of the theory as it provides a compelling and plausible account of the psychological maturational challenges that the very young infant has to encounter if they are to progress away from the primitive narcissistic state. It is a complementary model of development, does not contradict what we have seen so far, and can be used to illustrate very clearly how the impulse to revenge both defends the more primitive states from disintegration and, tragically, also inhibits maturation to more advanced and adaptive states.

Proceeding from original Kleinian ideas, Object Relations theory proposes that very early infant psychological development depends on a successful development through two stages. In normal development these stages are encountered and completed in the first year of life but remain present throughout life and can be re-activated at any time. The more primitive position is called the paranoid-schizoid position and the subsequent one, which depends for development upon adequate care giving, is the depressive position. We can see that these stages might be similar to the primary and secondary narcissistic stages and it is true, in the absence of some conceptual differences, that they are largely comparable in content and characteristic. It is also true to say that the progression from one stage to the next will depend chiefly upon identical qualities of care giving and likewise, development might be arrested by the same factors of neglect or trauma. The paranoid-schizoid position is considered to be the state of mind of the infant from birth to four to six months. The name describes its essential features: the 'paranoid' anxiety related to external threats and the internally projected threats that arise from the 'schizoid' feature of splitting people and objects into 'good' (gratifying, loving and loved) and 'bad' (frustrating, hated and persecutory). The 'bad', which as a result of the splitting process is wholly bad and potentially annihilating, is the inescapable source of anxiety.

We have already seen that although the price for splitting is paranoia and anxiety, it is necessary as a result of the fragility of the infants' undeveloped self. The fantasy protects the good from the bad, which would be impossible if they existed in the same place and time or in the same person. The progression to the secondary, depressive position is enabled by the support of a loving, tolerant and empathetic caregiver who encourages the infant to bring the 'good' and the 'bad' together and realise ambivalence. This manoeuvre also involves mourning the loss of the idealised, all good, omnipotent, person or self-image. A successfully negotiated mourning process is the key to forgoing primitive narcissism and enabling development out of the paranoid-schizoid position. In simple terms, it is the task of the caregiver to encourage and support this loss and mourning. In doing so, the care giver can help the infant to appreciate that the benefits of an authentic, though ambivalent and less than perfect, relationship might outweigh the comforts and refuge of primitive narcissism. If we recall chapter 8, we might remember that this is precisely the conclusion that TS Eliot appeared to be suggesting in 'The Cocktail Party'

On the other hand, faced with an inadequate, abusive or terrifying environment the infant may 'decide' to remain shrouded and protected by the illusions provided through the paranoid-schizoid state. The result we have seen; an orientation towards and a preference for taking refuge in primitive narcissism, together with an enduring and unassailable propensity to revengeful practice in defence of that narcissism. If, however, the infant perceives the environment and caregiving as essentially, or substantially, good it will choose to allow the natural development and move towards the second position; the 'depressive position'. The depressive position is characterised by mourning the loss of the perfect but also by an increasing capacity to integrate the good and the bad and tolerate an ambivalent and ordinary, real relationship. In being supported by the caregiver to engage with the depressive position, to experience mourning and depressive anxiety[6], the infant can learn to tolerate ambivalence, frustration and imperfection and develop the central defining feature of healthy adulthood: mixed feelings towards pretty much everything and everybody and a capacity to tolerate a 'good enough' life without raging against its imperfections. The support the caregiver can provide is, in essence, a gentle and compassionate teaching of the facts of life, the 'givens' of life and the limitations of ordinary human relationships. It is at this point that the child will learn either one or the other of the crucial, and life defining, lessons of life.

The child will either learn that bad feelings mean that someone is doing something wrong (stuck at the paranoid-schizoid stage) or that bad feelings do not necessarily mean that someone is doing something wrong and the feelings themselves may be assuaged through self-soothing and mutual empathetic support (advanced to the depressive position). The importance of making this transition successfully cannot be overstated as a continued attachment to the belief that bad feelings equals bad deeds is a hugely disabling characteristic if carried into adult life. On the other hand, to develop a belief that bad feelings do not necessarily equal bad deeds by is a blessing that will support the development of authentic, loving and sustainable relationships throughout life. Bad deeds can, and rightly should, be addressed through ethical and social mechanisms involving justice, punishment or reparation. However, bad feelings (that may or may not be the result of bad deeds) are more effectively addressed directly, responsibly and in the context of a personal narrative without the futile distraction of blame, accusation and schism and all the violence and hatred this will entail. The person who has generally negotiated their way well enough to the depressive position will understand that bad feelings can be borne and comforted directly through compassion and understanding and that pursuit of the wrongdoer only diverts and delays the necessary emotional processing of powerlessness, humiliation and loss that inevitably accompany the hurt. This maturing movement from the paranoid-schizoid position to the depressive radically alters the relationship style of the infant who now becomes increasingly aware of their separateness and ordinariness in respect of the twin poles of power and vulnerability. Indeed, the separating infant may come to realise that they now possesses the power to harm the caregiver whilst simultaneously recognising their vulnerability to needs for care and attention. Anxieties[6] might arise related to separateness and the capacity of the infant to influence this one way or the other. Hence, the infant begins to learn that they can both attract and repel the person they depend upon by their attitudes and behaviour.

This is the genesis of natural socialisation in that this secondary awareness will give rise to feelings such as guilt and loss and the wish to make good what has been harmed. The infant may also begin to develop feelings of gratitude that can be a counterweight, tempering the primitive feelings, to aggression and envy. In this way the foundations of mutually supportive, loving and empathetic adult relationships are laid. For a child negotiating this stage of development their characteristic behaviour can alternate alarmingly between cruel and rejecting behaviour and loving, reparative behaviour. Such behaviour reflects a deeper ambivalence about the transitional phase as the child oscillates for a time between the two positions. The caregiver faces a massive challenge to help the young person find the middle ground without resorting to their own acts of retaliation or revenge in some way. Further development can result in a sophisticated capacity for empathy that can develop as the forerunner of complex feelings of love and fidelity. Such an enormous milestone can then lead to more development increasing empathy, sympathy and concern for the experience of others.

As the psychic impact of primitive narcissism and paranoid-schizoid mechanisms diminish there will be corresponding decrease in split destructive projections. Differentiation between inner and outer worlds becomes more adaptive, tolerable and accurate. If all goes well, we can see that the protective mechanisms of the primitive states (omnipotence, splitting, solipsistic orientations and paranoia) are increasingly redundant as the child gradually values the benefits of ordinary and imperfect life, and ordinary relationships, over an omnipotent, yet wholly imaginary and fragile, one. Melanie Klein described the experience of moving towards the depressive position: 'My contention is that the child goes through states of mind comparable to the mourning of the adult' and further, 'this early morning is revived whenever grief is experienced later in life[8]'.

Attachments to fantasies of revenge are an avoidance of the work of mourning the omnipotent self. Revenge is indeed a lazy form of grief. A grief for the dead or dying part of the omnipotent self that has for so long been a comfort and refuge in an imagined, or real, hostile and capricious world. The difficult work of psychotherapy with the chronically entranced revenger is to invite and encourage this mourning process. The psychotherapeutic work aims to re-animate and complete a penetrating narcissistic mortification[8] in an informed, unhurried, empathetic and sensitive way and at a pace that the client can bear without psychological splitting. The almost irresistible temptation to return to the refuge of the primitive state will be ever present throughout the process.

It is worth noting that, as adults, we are neither in the position of having grown up and attained the depressive position, nor in the position of failing to do so. It is not an either/or proposition. A more realistic assessment would be to see the transformation from paranoid-schizoid to depressive positions as an endless game of snakes and ladders. Each one of us is more or less poised in a precarious balance between the two and dependent for the outcome of that balance on a combination of constitutional, developmental and environmental factors over which we, as children, had little control. In the paranoid-schizoid position, the maintenance of a revengeful relationship functions to side-step unbearable knowledge of human frailty and limitations and avoid the work of mourning the loss of illusion. If we can be harmed then we cannot be omnipotent unless we can return the harm and all the associated feelings, like for like. Otherwise, we must face ourselves as ordinary, mortal and vulnerable human beings. The awful truth is that, in the face of ordinary mortality, we can be overpowered and harmed by things over which we have no control; 'they' can get away with it and there is nothing we can do to stop them. Powerlessness, humiliation and loss.

This state of affairs is unimaginable for a person who is already emotionally vulnerable and needs at all costs to protect and maintain a precarious internal psychological equilibrium. The revenger's essential statement is 'this cannot happen to me'. The statement of the ordinary mortal who has transcended the narcissistic challenge would be 'sometimes this can and will happen to me and it will hurt and may cause me to lose something very important'. The meaning of 'me' in each statement is crucially different: the revenger's 'me' is the 'me' of the fragile narcissistic, paranoid-schizoid state whereas the 'me' of the ordinary mortal is supported by the blessings of the depressive position and all the flexibility, maturity and realism of an endurable, imperfect, ambivalent, yet tolerant and secure enough self.

We saw in Chapter 5 that the psychological consequence of an evolutionarily emergent consciousness of the self is self-significance. 'I' have value and significance over and above my organic significance and the price we pay for this significance is anxiety. The psychotherapeutic models we have so far examined are, at root, concerned with how we respond to this anxiety for good or ill, the consequences this has on our human relationships and how we might set about fixing things when severe distress and anxiety become a chronic feature of our lives. This is the business of psychotherapy. Psychotherapeutic theory and practice has revealed a plausible connection between anxiety and the conflicting demands of anxious illusion vs. ordinary, limited relationships, together with the necessity of resolving this psychological conundrum. In this book, I have tried to demonstrate the ways that human beings have mistakenly employed the revenge scenario to try and side-step this developmental challenge, with devastating consequences.

Anxiety manifests when we feel a disquieting loss of omnipotence and a dread about the vulnerability we and our loved ones face in the real world. In respect of the object relational model of human development, ordinary (or depressive) anxiety can be adaptive and encourage maturation. In contrast to paranoid anxiety, which results in splitting and refuge from the world, maturational anxiety is part of mourning. 'Depressive (mourning) anxiety' is consequent upon the transition to the depressive position and is the essential element of all mature relationships. It is the ground from which empathy, generosity, altruism, and gratitude and forbearance spring and through this, love both for self and others. It comes from the awareness that although anxiety is a given of life, it need not be unbearable where it exists within a supportive environment. Anxiety becomes bearable and digestible if it can be mutually shared in empathy, love and compassion. The balm and comfort that can be provided by a loving, empathetic and tolerant care giver during the period of mourning for the lost omnipotent self is the critical component in 'joining the ordinary human race' and infants and children who receive enough of this are given a gift of decisive consequence. Those who are deprived of this gift will be caught in the grip of perplexing and destructive narcissistic responses and a propensity to engage in great harm through initiating repeated revenge scenarios. Most of us will find ourselves located between these two poles and be propelled one way or the other by the winds of fortune and the relative limits of what we've had, what we've done and what we have become.

From the psychotherapist's point of view it is useful to remind ourselves about the kitten under the sofa. The kitten under the sofa, although afraid to come out, desires to come out and has an organically, genetically programmed drive to come out. So it is with the dynamics of primary narcissism and the paranoid-schizoid position in that we are likewise programmed to psychologically progress away from them to the mature position. This is most certainly advantageous to the therapeutic endeavour even though learned anxieties and the resultant life experiences might have held a person in regression for many years. It is an organic fact that life processes will persist in pushing towards their innate pre-determined paths even though individual patterns of fear-induced somatic, emotional and cognitive restrictions are rigidly in place. The psychotherapeutic process is aiming for a gentle and compassionate long-delayed death of the narcissistically oriented self. With the fictional client I wish to present, complex and well-founded overwhelming fears maintained an unhappy stasis for many years which, along with the mourning process, prevented such a death.

Peter was 52 when he first came to see me complaining of feelings of despair, penetrating loneliness, lethargy and an intense misanthropic orientation towards the world. He was single and had no significant friends. He worked alone as a self-employed clock maker and repairer, from which he made a subsistence level income. He had no interest in his work other than as source of income. He lived with his mother in a small house that had been built by his father. He told me at our first meeting, forcefully and with pronounced bitterness, that his father had ensured that neither he nor his mother would inherit this house following his death. His father had indeed died the previous year and Peter and his mother were contesting the estate but remained at some risk of homelessness. In response to what he saw as his father's final betrayal from beyond the grave, Peter was extremely bitter and angry and felt utterly helpless and defeated. He described his father as a 'complete and utter bastard' and his mother as intimidated and abused by him. Peter was deeply disappointed that his father's death had not enabled his mother to 'come alive' as he had hoped she would do. During our first meeting, Peter spoke in alternating tones of wronged and defeated victimhood and vicious vengefulness. More than once it struck me that he was potentially a dangerously violent man although he assured me that he had never acted on his florid misanthropic fantasies.

Peter had a brother who had been two years older than him. He described his brother as an 'animal' who would not 'take any shit from anybody' and was capable of extreme and viciously vengeful violence. He was feared in the local community, had a reputation as a dangerous man, a criminal record for assault and regularly engaged in vendettas, which he would pursue with pitiless hatred. Peter spoke in an animated way about his brother, admired his violent prowess and yet had been fearful of him and passively hateful and envious. His brother had committed suicide three years earlier, by intentionally crashing his car and Peter wondered if he might do the same as it appeared to him to be a heroic and exciting way to die. He expressed other vague suicidal thoughts but had no plans or definite intentions. In fact, Peter's fantasies generally had strong homicidal elements, rather than suicidal. My initial feeling was of concern for his suffering, together with a wariness about his capacity for hatred. I felt some personal dislike for his insistence that he was prey to a terrible injustice. Peter based his identity on his victimhood and entitlement to reparation. On many occasions, he romanticised the fact of his victimhood and suggesting a heroic quality to his survival into adulthood.

Peter's relationship with his ex-military father had been a humiliating and violent experience. Many times during his psychotherapy sessions Peter would re-tell stories of his father's violent and heroic achievements in the army and, as with his brother's exploits, was both admiring and fearful of these. His father was ruthlessly authoritative, demanded submission from his family and would enforce this with outbursts of sudden and shocking violence. He was a hard-hearted man, a heavy drinker and highly unpredictable. Peter also told me that occasionally they would have fun together, a day out or gifts, generosity and warmth in the household for periods of time. Peter was afraid of his father but also disdainful of his need for violence which, despite his envy, he saw as a weakness. He was envious of his father's ability to dominate through violence and coveted his standing in the community as a man not to be messed with. He was glad when his father died and claimed not to miss him. On the other hand, Peter spoke lovingly of his elderly mother and said he wished to care for her and ensure no more harm came to her. It had not always been so as Peter described an adoringly seductive, yet alternately vicious and annihilating, woman for whom Peter was both a comfort and a burden. She told him openly that she had not wanted him, another child, and would have terminated the pregnancy if she had not been afraid of her husband's reaction. He felt that he was, in truth, her favourite child and she would often confide to him about her marital frustrations. She was alternately adoring and unpredictably viciously annihilating, chiefly through physical and sexual humiliation and in comparing him unfavourably to 'real men'. In the moments when she was, in his terms, 'loving' his mother would heap praise on him and relate very improbable fantasies about his specialness, his superiority and spin tales of the greatness he would achieve. Such occasions were combined with a sexually charged physical proximity, falling short of overt sexual activity, and the combination created a promise-laden, tenacious and exceptionally ambivalent relationship. This bond was apparent to the rest of the family and served to exacerbate the hostility from both the father and the brother towards Peter.

Peter's relationship with his brother involved a wary, distant admiration although Peter remembered that he always wanted to be close to his brother. He spoke of how his brother had bullied and tormented him, without pity, and had revelled in a sadistic exploitation of Peter's dependency on him. Thus, their relationship was characterised by longing and dependency on Peter's part, which was met with violent, crushing humiliation and sadistic bullying. Neither parent would intervene claiming that it was 'for the two boys to sort out'. On one occasion, Peter did react with rage and his own torrent of violence. This resulted in his brother's hospitalisation and Peter's running away from home for three days in fear of retribution.

It was apparent from our first meetings that Peter had no experience of a reliable and consistent positive relationship and thus, the likelihood of his emerging into adaptive adult relationships was minimal. Indeed, his experiences of intimacy chiefly involved violence and his characteristic relationship style, as revealed in his storytelling and in our relationship, was predominantly maintained by a hateful longing. Much later in our meetings Peter told me that he also had a sister, some 12 years older than him and that she had run away at the age of 15 saying she wanted nothing more to do with any of them. He always carried a photograph of his 15 year-old sister but did not know where she was, or if she was still alive. His memory of his sister was that she was nice to him, her baby brother, and yet there were elements here too of a teasing humiliation combined with vague sexual allure.

Peter's infancy and childhood contained all the elements likely to result in a high risk that his emotional and psychological development would manifest in the very situation we referred to in chapter 8: 'that the stories we make up and tell about ourselves are infinitely preferable to the stories that might be told by a dispassionate observer'. This was indeed the case and when I met him at the age of 52, the consequences of his failure to adequately negotiate the narcissistic challenge were painfully apparent. He was in the grip of a deeply entrenched way of life wherein the totality of his satisfactions came from highly developed grandiose fantasies of domination and imaginary triumphant deeds bringing him fame, glory and adoration, particularly from women. His sexual activity was, and always had been, solitary masturbation accompanied by lurid and violent fantasy. He had no interest in women other than in a fantasy of adoring submission to his desires, combined with domination and violent abuse. His relationships with men were exclusively violently competitive although characterised by an outward display of humility and submission.

Peter employed elaborate and hidden fantasies of omnipotence and supremacy and imagined the successful execution of violent and sadistic acts of revenge. Such acts would be rehearsed endlessly in his mind and he would gain enormous pleasure from them. The stories he told himself would always remain in the sphere of the imaginary as he lacked the courage to externalise them, fearing retribution. He did derive satisfaction and relief from these tales, but of an autoerotic or masturbatory kind. They needed to be endlessly repeated. Like an encroaching tide, the pressure of the reality of his self and life was forever threatening to destabilise and destroy his grandiose but fragile narcissistic equilibrium. Repetition and reinforcement of illusion temporarily held back the tide. Increases in the urgency, content and degree of imaginary violent omnipotence would always occur following his perception of receiving insults or slights from people around him. Alarmingly, to my mind, such 'insults' could be utterly trivial but still be capable of triggering a cascade of venomous, hateful and revengeful imaginings.

Characteristic of our relationship was his need to narrate these fantasies to me in exquisite detail, together with corresponding fantasies of grandiose achievement and dominion. In his fantasy he was insistent that he was in fact a man of great potency, dominant and intellectually masterful. Like the literary revengers, Vindice and Iago, he sought adoration from his audience. In a further grandiose elaboration he would claim that the reason he did not act out these fantasies was because he had no wish to 'descend to their level'. In this way even his humiliation was translated to a source of pride and something to be admired. It was clear that he wished me to see him not as he appeared to the world but as the potent, dominant, avenging and righteous man he wished himself to be. He wanted me to see Peter the super-avenger, rather than Peter the beaten and humiliated man.

As might be guessed, Peter was a highly dysfunctional man with an almost complete functional impotency in all areas of his outward life. His imaginary rehearsals of revenge and domination gratified him to the extent that they could reconstitute his crumbling solipsistic, narcissistic self. Gratification resulted from repeating, time and time again, rescuing and refashioning his grandiose illusions that were continually being eroded by life events. He played the triumphant saviour to his illusory self (the only self he had) over and over and experienced this with something like orgasmic relief.

Peter and I worked together without much progress for a number of years, except that he derived some empathetic support and relief from his anxiety. I was unable to negotiate a fruitful way to reach beyond the bitterness and desire for revenge to the profound vulnerability that I thought to be there. With regard to his deeper narcissistic issues, I found him to be unapproachable and expressions of concern, direct or indirect, towards the fraught little boy I assumed him to have been would be met with blankness and immediately followed by a tirade of hatred against his present day tormentors. In speaking directly to the hurt boy in him, I was provoking contact with the terribly vulnerable emotions he was unable to safely experience. As was the case in the family I wrote about in chapter 1, expressions of positive and empathetic human contact towards Peter would always be met with hostility and an increase of imaginary violence. This was done in order to keep at arm's length the deeper and almost forgotten needs for comfort and solace in fear that such feelings would break through the carapace of hatred and overwhelm him completely.

It was something of a puzzle that this hatred was rarely, if ever, discharged openly towards me and I wondered aloud on one occasion why it might be that he hardly ever attacked me. Peter paused and smiled and, in a halting and hesitant voice, went on to make a startling revelation about his relationship with me. He told me that he was determined to remain miserable, to frustrate all attempts at therapeutic progress and to spoil my reputation and standing as a psychotherapist. He saw me as arrogant and self-satisfied but also knew from his investigations in the local community that I was well thought of and respected as an effective psychotherapist. He experienced my observations as presumptuous and humiliating. The very fact that he needed help was deeply insulting to his omnipotence. He felt my attempts to change him as playing God and 'who did I think I was to even think he would submit'. He was determined to prove his dominion and omnipotence by defeating me, humiliating me and facing me with my impotence and failure. His reasoning was quite specific and he often brooded on his ultimate victory over me and savoured the moment at some future time when the decisive humiliation and contrition would be revealed. He was such a special person, such a difficult case, that to become 'well' would allow me to claim the glory and adoration he so desired himself. His revenge was to deny this to me and thereby reveal his superiority in triumph. There was a clear reference to the admired suicide of the brother although he, apparently, wanted to go one better and take someone with him.

Whilst all this was potentially threatening, I was reassured by the knowledge that he had no history of ever acting on his fantasies and they had always remained as illusion. I became aware that he had been acting out this fantasy for some time, secretly defeating me and yet, the fact of him revealing his revenge on me suggested a shift in our relationship. Previously, for Peter to brood in isolation on a story had been as good, if not better, than the actuality. Here he was sharing this story with me, risking deconstruction of the myth by exposing it to the reality of another person. The fact that he was revealing his direct, personal revenge fantasy indicated a shift in the dynamics of that fantasy and possibly a maturity emerging in his relationship with me. Never before had he shared his fantasies so directly in the immediacy of a relationship and in the telling I sensed a swing towards me as a real, separate, person rather than simply a player in his internal drama.

As we have seen, such shifts are the initial stages of the maturation of the primitive narcissistic state and the courageous first steps in relinquishing the refuge it provides. Fortunately, Peter's revelation of his latent desires for revenge towards me did reflect a deeper positive regard for our relationship and the presence of a maturing impulse. It was he who had chosen to reveal himself in this way, risking possible retaliation together with the loss of the fantasy and the comfort and refuge it had previously provided. Our work together subsequently allowed a careful approach to the latent hatred and grandiosity that had so far concealed his terrors. The unfolding of this element of our relationship gradually exposed some of the roots of the narcissistic/revenge dynamic, which were so present and locked in Peter's personality and had condemned him to his lonely and tormented way of life. It became possible for him to own and examine other aspects of his grandiosity and illusions of omnipotence and his hidden desires. He desired, at all costs, to defend the absolute 'goodness' of himself and, tragically, to destroy anything that might be good outside of himself. He began to see his propensity for envious, revengeful behaviour and more importantly, to begin to tolerate some of the previously unbearable feelings that lay beneath.

One session I remember well. We were in the middle of a heated dispute about some aspect of the rights and wrongs of someone's behaviour. I believe it was a quarrel about interpretation; Peter taking a characteristically paranoid view and my view being more (irritatingly) benign. Peter accused me of arrogance and having a 'know it all' attitude. We danced around these accusations for a while and my thought was to bring it to a close by owning, admitting my propensity for arrogance and how it had been triggered by our talking together. I decided to share with Peter an understanding of my need for arrogance, my sense of the narcissism that underpinned it and the need to defend myself by projecting this 'fault' onto him. I tried to explain how I sometimes also needed to take this stand, in effect saying, 'I am right and you are wrong and furthermore, it is you who are being arrogant about it.'

I rarely make this kind of intervention and it carried the risk of appearing to Peter to be too real and too soon, thus unsettling him enough to return to his refuge. Fortunately, throughout our time together, I had become enough of a safe object to enable Peter to cautiously move away from his primitive narcissism and receive what I was saying as a description of myself (and not him) and as an invitation to move a little further. My disclosure startled him but enabled Peter to start to take back some of his own projections and show an interest in his own needs for arrogance and grandiosity. At this point, we were able to begin the careful work of deconstructing the illusory edifice that had been his only sanctuary for 50 years. His fear and his emotional experience was that in the absence of his illusions, he was nothing. This was far from a straight path, more like a spiral continually turning back on itself, (like Klein's snakes and ladders) but overall moving slowly forward into ordinary life, towards ordinary people and ordinary relationships. We were able to continue in this spirit for some time and eventually Peter came face to face with his own human ordinariness, a realistic view of his potency and potential and his capacity for achieving his desires within the givens of his particular life. Indeed, Peter discovered that he was far less than ordinary in some ways, and in some ways quite disabled. With great sadness and disappointment he set about reviewing the actuality of his life and his achievements. The gentle scouring that was the mourning process began and its wake revealed the ground upon which he began to reassemble a more realistic view of himself and his potency. The mourning involved in this process was vast and he indulged the temptation to return to anger and blame for temporary relief many times. It was a very difficult time for Peter and suicidal thoughts returned more than once, although in grief and not in the guise of a heroic act.

Over the next months, he experienced terrible grief at the loss of his specialness, at the disappointment of ordinary life and above all, an overwhelming sorrow and ennui for the broken and abandoned promises of his imaginary life. However, correspondingly, his misanthropy diminished along with some of his chronic and intense desires to engage in revenge dramas. People no longer did things wrong all the time, his paranoia lessened and when things did go wrong or he was disappointed or hurt, let down and betrayed, he was able to respond as if this were a painful but ordinary and bearable part of life. No longer did he believe something, or someone, was evil just because he was feeling bad. His primitive narcissism diminished to a manageable level and his day-to-day addiction to revenge practically disappeared. He remained a man with a strong propensity to revenge when stressed, or when he felt himself slighted in some way, but he was now able to 'catch himself in the act' and draw back his impulse. Although he still felt the impulse he also felt himself to have a choice over whether he indulged it or not. In some ways, he came to see himself not as master of the world, but of his own internal impulses. Towards the end of our work together he told me that he thought his impulse to revenge, while immensely satisfying and comforting, was a mistake in exactly the same way that drinking a bottle of whiskey a day was a mistake.

Peter is a fictional composite of many people I have worked with. In telling his story, I have tried to present a picture of the narcissistic state as it impacts on an individual's life. In particular, I have shown how this manifests behaviourally as an unassailable preference for revenge dynamics to defend the fragility of the underlying vulnerability. That this man had been engaged in his circular, self-generating and self-reinforcing mistake for almost 50 years is a testament to both its addictive promise of redemption and its ultimate futility. When Peter first came to see me, he was sick of his life and yet could find no comfort other than to continue doing the things he had been doing in the forlorn hope of a different outcome.

The nature of primitive narcissism is that it is self-referencing and recognises no reality other than the illusions it relies on for existence. The narcissistic state has no capacity for external verification and violently defends itself against incursions of external reality that threaten to destabilise its integrity and absolute hold on the personality. Peter was someone caught in this nightmare and the devastating impact it had had on his life and relationships to was all too apparent. His extensive and continuous use of revengeful imagination was the most effective means he had of providing some comfort and stability in his precarious existence. His continual assertion that someone had done something wrong, together with the accompanying stabilising, focussed hatred and desires to pay back the feelings that were so unbearable were the only way he knew to avoid further disintegration. His hatred stabilised his fragmented self in a way that nothing else appeared to be able to do. Previously, to stop generating hatred would plunge him into a psychological abyss. It would make him lose face in plain view of his brutal self-criticism and his imaginary cruel and humiliating, unforgiving, audience. The disintegration of his necessary grandiose illusion, together with the ensuing chaos and loss of control, had generated such terror of annihilation of his fragile hold on himself to make it, literally, unthinkable.

I now know that, in this particular instance the solution to chronic and immutable impulses to revenge was found in the realm of narcissistic mortification, the death of primitive narcissism and the birth of ordinary human curiosity in imperfect, fellow people. Mortification of the primitive narcissism undertaken over a period of years carried out (imperfectly) with precision, patience, non-retaliation when hurt and a willingness to engage in authentic dialogue with empathy and compassion. This is not re-parenting but a supported, deep mourning process that tries to accommodate the limitations we are presented with at whatever stage of life. Narcissistic mortification leaves in its wake a devastated landscape of shattered illusion and it can be difficult at that stage to see what might make this worthwhile. When Peter and I finally parted company he still had not fully made up his mind whether he wanted what seemed to be available to him following the death of his narcissistic self. It looked very ordinary and bleak to him at times. I remain hopeful he would find a way to feel that ordinary life might be good enough.

CHAPTER ELEVEN

...and let them get away with it

In this final chapter I want to move away from discourse and argument and make some personal observations that have arisen from my experience as a psychotherapist over the last 25 years. For some years now I have offered workshops for people interested in the subject of revenge and when I'm asked for my solution to the problem of revenge and impulses to revenge, I will say that the answer is to let them get away with it. Given the foregoing ten chapters I hope that this statement is not as unacceptable as it might have been. I also hope that there is an appreciation of why I might be suggesting this as an emotionally sustainable and justly transformative solution. The therapeutic challenge thus presented is therefore: how can I let them get away with it, how can I bear to do this and how can I resolve, in a real and sustainable way, the feelings that will arise if I am to do this? I think I have shown that my answer to this lies with the slow, psychologically informed, compassionate mortification of the primary narcissistic state and not in the realms of justice, forgiveness, or superior ethical reasoning and reparation.

Thoughts and impulses to revenge spring from painful emotional and psychological remnants that remain in the human psyche even following due process of justice, punishment and reparation. Where justice is overlooked or not available, these remnants will be all the greater but it remains that, where they do exist, such remnants are not wholly extinguished by the execution of fair and appropriate ethical justice. Impulses to revenge, as I have defined them, arise from the irrational vicissitudes of self-importance and self-esteem and not from the imperatives of ethics and rationality. For the revenge scenario to be set in motion there is no need for an ethically proscribed wrong to have taken pace. There need be no offence or betrayal, no illegal act and nobody needs to have done anything wrong. It is only necessary for the revenger to feel wronged and for the continued existence of the wrongdoing to impact adversely on the revenger's image of selfhood. As we have seen, the capacity to feel wronged differs between people in relation to individual narcissistic dynamics and feeling wronged is not the same as being wronged. There are, however, strong correlations between the tendency to feel wronged, the propensity to engage in revengeful thoughts and acts and the degree to which primitive narcissistic elements remain in the adult personality. Such primitive narcissistic elements remain as a defence against the mortification that would otherwise occur as an inevitable part of growing up. The impulse to revenge is an attempt to solve a profound intra-psychic personal crisis that has been triggered by feeling vulnerable to the hurts of others and consequent upon an inability to solve the crisis in any other way. That the personal crisis reflects a pre-existing vulnerability and fragility in the psyche, and that the impulse to revenge only serves to re-establish this pre-existing state, explains the ultimate futility and circularity of the revenge scenario in human affairs.

My view is that the cascading personal crisis, which is triggered by feeling wronged, can only be fully and sustainably resolved by addressing the underlying and pre-existing vulnerability. This means re-visiting and re-evaluating the psychological challenges of very early life. Here will be found the painful remnants of emotional experience and where it will finally be understood that intra-psychic distress has little to do with someone having done something wrong. Difficult as it is, if we can shift our attention away from the wrongdoing, and the wrongdoer, and towards what it is like to feel wronged there is a possibility of moving away from the absolute need not to let them get away with it. If we can stop pursuing others and, instead, be curious and compassionate about what is happening to ourselves it may be possible to let them get away with it. We may also be more able to effectively and sustainably manage the painful remnants of powerlessness, humiliation and loss. If we can attend directly to our emotional and psychological needs as wounded and hurt people, and less to how bad others have been, experience has shown me that getting away with it or not becomes a matter of indifference.

The determination that the chronic revenger will hold onto their 'drug of choice' has been described throughout this book and even the most willing and curious of 'wronged' people find difficulty in negotiating the necessary emotional challenges involved in shifting a propensity to revengeful acts. The necessary emotional challenge is nothing less than a process of intense and prolonged mourning. Mourning requires bearing what feels to be unbearable and generating a realistic view of the merits of the self and the consequent opportunities and limitations of life.

My original training as a psychotherapist was in relational Body Psychotherapy at the Chiron Centre[1] in west London and I remain partly informed and attached to both the technical and theoretical aspects of the time I spent there. In respect of working with chronic impulses to revenge, the body psychotherapist[2], armed with a cognitive analysis and the technical ability to work with the underlying narcissistic state, will also be in a position to attend to the somatic manifestations of the scenario. For example, it will be seen that prior to action, the revenger/client will be in a profound state of general physical muscular contraction and in the grip of an unbearable, cognitively ill-formed, state of anxiety that results in an overwhelming physical, yet undefined, impulse to do something. This impulse is violent in nature and leads to severe emotional discomfort, a dangerous irritability and commonly, objects being thrown or broken and harsh words being spoken. The wishful fantasy is that by externalising the torrent of discomfort, by evacuating it to the people and objects around us, the discomfort will be assuaged. We have seen that while this may indeed be true, it brings only temporary and partial relief.

The revenger is gripped by an acute necessity to relieve their desperately painful state and their conscious awareness will be consumed by this state the exclusion of all else. As these tremendous forces coalesce into thought, an idea will emerge and centre on a specific single thought - that of not letting them get away with it. Immediately, the revenger feels some prospect of relief, if only they can pay them back for what they have done. The awfulness of the state cannot be understated particularly, as is commonly found, they have already got away with it and there's nothing that the revenger can do to change this. Similarly, experience shows that once the cascade has reached this point, the impulses have developed to a point of no return and anything other than discharge is very difficult. Attempts to influence the client as this point through rational argument, or appeals to maturity, will only meet with a 'yes, but…' response. The therapist will only unhelpfully frustrate the impulse ('because you don't understand') and the impulse is highly likely to be discharged into the consulting room and at the person of the therapist. At this late stage, there is very little resource available to the client that may influence the impulse to a different course.

To be held in the grip of an impulse to revenge is a deeply unpleasant experience yet, as I have shown, to evacuate this sensation does little more than re-establish an already fragile narcissistic state that leaves the individual vulnerable to future breakdowns. I have found that it is helpful to move towards the ability to use the resources of the body to internally process the drive toward evacuation. In essence, this involves attempting to arrest, and possibly reverse, the physical process that initiates the cascade of internal devastation and ultimately revengeful action. This is most difficult to achieve as it involves 'catching' the impulse at its earliest stages (where it may potentially be modified) before it cascades and becomes both unbearable and invincible. The process requires a considerable degree of activity on the part of the psychotherapist, involving both interruptions and physical promptings that may be unusual, or uncomfortable, for many therapists. The client will be in a state of sympathetic nervous system arousal in the same way as they would be when faced with a personal threat and, in the absence of interruption, will habitually discharge that arousal in thoughts and acts of revenge. Such interruptions that the therapist might make present the client with an opportunity to consider and experiment with alternatives to violent evacuation. Instructions, and physical promptings to change patterns of breathing, chronic muscular contractions and physical posturing would be indicated where the therapist watches carefully for the beginnings of the cascade during the narrative of the client. Gross signs, such as irritability or general muscular contraction, can be noticed and commented upon and physical promptings may be used to interrupt the cascade. More subtle signs revealed by the autonomic nervous system[3], moving towards readiness for action and into the 'pre-evacuation' state, may also be attended to and interrupted subtly, by word or deed on the part of the therapist. These interruptions are designed to arrest the cascade and have the therapeutic intention of encouraging the client to feel directly what the cascade is designed to stop them feeling. In other words, if it is possible to arrest the cascade towards hatred then powerlessness, humiliation and grief may become available to other therapeutic intervention. The therapist can only then begin to work, not with the client's grievance but, with their grief.

If we picture the body as an inflated balloon then it is possible to demonstrate a very simple model of emotional functioning together with a model of neurosis. In a state of relaxed equilibrium the pressure inside the balloon holds the equilibrium of the balloon to a degree of expansion that is neither too much nor too little. Neither too much nor too little means that it is held in state producing a subjective feeling of relaxed yet alert equilibrium, a feeling of wellbeing (assuming the balloon, like the person, has self-aware feelings). We might say that the material that the balloon is made of is stretched to its optimum extent and the pressure inside the balloon is likewise at the optimum required for all the life functions to operate well inside it. Inside the balloon are all the materials needed for the physical processes of life and the self-regulatory mechanisms. The self-regulatory mechanism we are particularly interested in is the one I have called the life of the emotions. As we saw in Chapter 6, the emotions are one of the self-regulatory mechanisms of the body in that they respond to environmental and internal changes and automatically adapt the body accordingly. We also saw in the same chapter that the emotions are more complex in that, being perceived by a self-conscious human being, they also derive a narrative meaning that goes above and beyond purely organic need. In other words, of all the systems of the body, the emotional system is the one that has feelings and also, the one we have feelings about. For example, when we are digesting food or increasing our heart rate running up the stairs we do not commonly have feelings about this (unless it hurts). However, when our body is responding to a physical threat by increasing our heart rate we may well impose a whole narrative on this phenomenon. For example, our heart rate increasing as we run up the stairs will induce a very different narrative meaning to an increasing heart rate caused by running from a burning building. In the second example, the narrative we generate will most likely have our self-significance as the central feature and furthermore, the resulting narrative will progress the narrative meaning still further.

Returning to the balloon. The stimulation of a meaning inducing narrative consequent upon changes in organic phenomena may be seen as increasing the internal pressure of the balloon/organic self. The system can respond in many ways to this and the way it responds will be highly influenced by both the narrative we have generated and by the historically structured (neurotic) reflexes of the balloon/person. One possibility is that the balloon can stretch temporarily to accommodate the increase in pressure until the self-regulating mechanisms inside the balloon work to reduce the pressure and allow the system to return to its previous state of equilibrium. An example of this would be where a person has a mild emotional response to a memory – perhaps a vague ennui resulting from a lost love or a warm feeling of happiness at remembering a pleasurable event. The expansion of the balloon in this case might be a simple intake of breath in order to accommodate the physical changes wrought by the feeling of the memory and the biochemical changes that will simultaneously occur. Such events happen to all of us dozens of times every day and present no challenge to our self-regulatory capabilities.

Alternatively, a stronger emotional event might produce an increase in pressure inside the balloon that cannot be accommodated by the internal mechanisms and, in this case, some active expression will be required in order to fully self-regulate. The pressure inside the balloon stretches the skin of the balloon to the extent that it becomes uncomfortable or even painful to tolerate. In this instance, the system can make use of the design feature of the balloon in that it has a valve for letting off pressure into the external atmosphere. Human beings have just such valves in the form of expressive functions and these are very effective at reducing uncomfortable and painful states. The human self-regulating system is much more sophisticated than a simple balloon but can function in the same way by discharging excess internal pressure and thereby attempt to restore the desired comfortable equilibrium. We can physically move our bodies, we can speak, we can shout, we can hit, we can cry and we can seek solace and comfort from other people.

We can also, as we have seen, act in ways that attempt to self-regulate but, because of misunderstandings and unhelpful habitual responses stemming from our childhood, don't fully work or work only to the degree that they re-instate a previously distorted and vulnerable system. The important thing to appreciate is that any emotional event, beyond something of very mild and benign stimulus, produces a pressure in the body that is felt as discomfort and an impulse to express this excess pressure will naturally follow. This will be the case even if we have no idea what the emotion is and, in such a case, the outcome can be a general anxiety that constantly seeks discharge. In this sense, we can understand anxiety not as a feeling in itself but as a result of some other, unspecified, feeling being left unexpressed. The healthy child will move towards an ability to manage their emotions like the balloon, either by internal processing and self-soothing or by expressing them into relationship with empathetic and loving other people who may offer support, encouragement and, if necessary, solace.

The healthy model of emotional functioning I am proposing requires a reasonably flexible balloon with some capacity for internal self-regulation. Furthermore, when the limits of the internal self-regulation are reached by the degree of passion triggered by the emotional event the (healthy) balloon has a fearless ability to discharge emotional residue as necessary into relationship with others. This relationship enables the system to regulate through the mutuality of empathy, compassion and shared experience in a way that cannot be achieved alone. It is the free and full functioning of these mechanisms of self-regulation, both alone and in relationship, which are the key to health, rather than a capacity to either endure or avoid the painful vagaries of life. In order that resolution of injury, hurt and harm done, be true and sustainable it must proceed from self-regulatory principles. It will not come from heightened and rigidly enforced resilience and organic repression nor, from the relentless pursuit and paying back of the wrongdoer.

Unfortunately, the person whose personality is subject to unmodified and primitive narcissistic imperatives has a balloon of a very different type. The processes I described that result in primitive narcissistic elements gaining ascendency in the adult personality will determine the person's capacity to tolerate and accommodate emotional experience in a profoundly detrimental way. The 'narcissistic' balloon has a very inflexible skin, a marked inability to process painful states within itself and painfully limited and rigid mechanisms for expression and discharge. As a consequence, such a person does not have the ability to expand as the internal pressure rises in response to an emotional event and as their capacity for self-soothing relies on one rigidly habitual manoeuvre – fragmentation and the creation and maintenance of illusion – there is very little functional stability. All emotional events will be dealt with in the same way. All emotions will be managed in accord with the structural limitations of the malformed and dysfunctional balloon. As internal pressure rises there can only be a combination of internal fragmentation, splitting and, where this is not sufficient, violent discharge. Fragmentation results from denial and splitting and from a disassociation of internal illusion from external reality. Internal and external violence is employed in the service of protecting and maintaining the fragmentation. The narcissistically fragile self is an inflexible vessel and cannot accommodate new our contradictory experience, nor can it tolerate threats to its essential self-sustaining illusions. It cannot expand to accommodate increased emotional pressure instead, almost as a reflexive action, it spits out new experience in the form of projection, employing all the forces of aggression at its disposal. Any new experience that requires a flexible alteration to the image of self will be perceived as an insult and a wrongdoing by the other. It is from this inflexibility and inability to accommodate the externals of life that the impulse to revenge emanates. Furthermore, tragically, it is this very same inflexibility and the associated, distorted defensive manoeuvrings that the impulse to revenge seeks to re-establish.

The container that is the balloon of the habitual revenger is a container of great rigidity and wholly incapable of accommodating the caprice and ordinary distress or the joys of life. The revenger builds an almost impenetrable wall of illusion around themselves that is defended with paranoid violence and maintained by the unshakable conviction that someone's done something wrong. It is the work of psychotherapy to attempt to influence and modify this container and not to debate ethics. For the psychotherapist to become entangled in the client's assertion that they've been wronged, and to focus on the wrongdoing, is a dangerous distraction from the task. Indeed, my experience has shown me that the more I engage in ethics, or hold an opinion as to the right and wrongs of the client's situation the less therapeutic I will be. In other words, for me there is a clear and convincing correlation between the therapist taking an ethical stance regarding the facts of the client's life and a failure to carry out the therapeutic task. The stronger my ethical opinion, the less therapeutic

I will be. It is the business of others (including the client) to consider the 'right thing'. The business of the therapist lies with the internal state of the client, their capacity for self-regulation and, above all, taking a critical view regarding instrumental errors in emotional regulation and in thinking and behaving. The task of therapy lies in the attempt to establish in the revenger a capacity for self-regulation through both self-soothing and through authentic and empathic intimate mutuality with themselves and other human beings. I would suggest that this is most fruitfully established through an attempt to reach an authentic and intimate empathic mutuality within themselves. Unfortunately, these are the very things which the revenger will view with extreme prejudice and suspicion hence, the enormity of the task.

My experience is that it is not an impossible task and it is worth remembering that everything the chronic revenger will tell us about themselves, including their belief that they can't bear certain feelings is, in some ways, an illusion. As a psychotherapist, I need not only to be disentangled from the client's assertion of victimhood but also to believe that their 'balloon' can be more flexible than they think it to be, or allow it to be. It is true that, in childhood, we do not have the capacity to bear extremes of painful emotion and will both split ourselves off from those things and from the experience of them. If this rigidity and absence of capacity for self-soothing persists, unmodified, into adulthood it can be severely disabling. Fortunately, in adulthood, the original defensive posture may be revisited, along with the additional emotional and intellectual resources of adulthood. There are many ways of achieving this and one way is to engage with the psychotherapeutic endeavour. The psychotherapist will focus their efforts on the functioning of the container, of the balloon, and not be distracted by the events of the client's life. Except in bearing witness, offering empathetic support and encouragement and in helping to understand the present situation the stories the client will tell are relevant only in what they tell us about the functioning of their regulatory capacities.

The adequate and healthy container, that is the self-conscious organic self, operates through the agency of three functional components: adequate flexibility in response to emotional events, a capacity for internal emotional self-regulation and self-soothing and, when simple internal self-regulation is not enough, a trust in and the ability to make use of relationships with others in mutual empathetic support. In this way, the uninterrupted emotional processes, the organically pre-determined self-regulatory mechanisms, may be able to gain ascendency over the early life compromises made in the service of defensiveness, schism and developmental arrest. Enmeshed in the complexities of therapeutic work, and given the infinite opportunities for distraction, it is sometimes difficult to remember that these three aspects of the human condition are the core concern of the psychotherapeutic endeavour. When left to get on with life, the human being is a wonderfully adept self-regulating organism. If we were better able to resist ingesting the injunctions and intrusions from self-imposed cultural power structures I think we would live much healthier, happier and less injurious lives. It seems to me that these power structures arise from essential, malignant, anxiety that has produced in our species a basic lack of faith in the processes of life and, in particular, faith in the organic self-regulatory importance of the emotions.

As a result of the consciousness of self we have ascribed a narrative meaning to our emotions that goes beyond the needs of the organic and, consequently, have feelings about those emotions. We have labelled our feelings as 'good feelings' or 'bad feelings'. As a result, we pursue some feelings and attempt to avoid others. We evaluate and ascribe personal meaning to our emotions, infuse them into the relative worth of human relationships and place them squarely at the centre of how we measure the meaningfulness and esteem of ourselves and our lives. In attempting to control our emotional states we have also lost a capacity for self-regulation and have neglected the processes that tend to encourage and support it. In many ways, the ascendancy of the rational human has been at the expense of the organic and impulsive and thus to the tragic neglect of the capacity of the human organism to self-regulate. To anxiously interfere with emotional process is to interfere with an essential self-regulatory mechanism and the result is all too often psychological, relational and physical ill-health. In the simplest terms possible, all the aberrant psychological phenomena we have examined throughout this book, the defence mechanisms, the splitting, the denials, diversions and narcissistic states begin with, and are maintained by, dysfunctional emotional self-regulation. We interfere with what we have come not to trust because it does not serve the excess elite needs for domination of others in repressive, hierarchical, power based cultural systems. Emotional autonomy remains a potent threat to established authority. Human society has developed largely through a wish to control and eliminate 'bad feelings' and the misery that is neurotic structuring in the personality stems from the ascendency of rapacious and repressive socialisation over organic function. The flexible, self-regulating and convivial balloon becomes the rigid, enduring, resilient and isolated balloon through a process of contraction against our own organic life process when, as children and adults, we are faced with fear of violence and the emotional and physical consequences of social castigation, humiliation and isolation.

Finally, I am aware of my tendency to repeat myself, which stems from my own neurotic structuring and attempts at self-regulation. However, I will do it one more time. My offering in this book is the perspective that if we are interested to arrest or mitigate the constant and ubiquitous impulse to revenge in human affairs we would do well to look beyond ethics and past thoughts of right and wrong behaviour. We should go beyond external justice, punishment and reparation and look additionally to the vicissitudes of the human psyche. In particular, to consider the structure and operation of the narcissistic mechanisms that have been revealed by psychotherapeutic thinking, theory and endeavour. I do not deny that the external manifestations of violence, abuse and exploitation need to be addressed through the processes of ethics and thereby, community enforcement of containment, punishment, deterrence and reparation. Such structures are essential to the safe and harmonious functioning of society. However, in addition to these essential checks on behaviour, my strong contention is that, from an emotional and psychological perspective, such structural mechanisms are wholly inadequate to prevent the persistence of the revenge scenario in human affairs.

Notes and Further Reading

Chapter One

1. Count Lev Nikolayevich Tolstoy; 9th September, 1828 to 20th November, 1910. Also known as Leo Tolstoy, was one of the giants of Russian literature. His works include the novels, War and Peace and Anna Karenina and novellas such as Hadji Murad and The Death of Ivan Ilyich. He was a prolific essayist, noted for his complicated and paradoxical persona and for his radical moralistic and ascetic views, which he adopted after a moral crisis and spiritual awakening in the 1870's.
2. A psychological manoeuvre is an integral protective mechanism that operates by translating distressing emotional experience into a more benign and bearable form. It does this by blocking the feeling element and by giving a new, more acceptable meaning to the experience. Whilst this might be correctly viewed as a distortion of reality, it is essentially a healthy and necessary part of how we cope with anxiety and stress. It is one of the most basic and indispensable ways we look after ourselves.
3. Mr Bumble is a fictional character in the novel Oliver Twist (1837–39) by Charles Dickens and is the cruel, pompous beadle of the poorhouse where the orphaned Oliver is raised.
4. Hindley Earnshaw is a fictional character in Emily Brontë's novel Wuthering Heights. The brother of Catherine Earnshaw, father of Hareton Earnshaw and sworn enemy of Heathcliff, he descends into a life of drunkenness, degradation, and misery after his wife Frances dies from consumption.

Chapter Two

1. Psychotherapy is a general term which refers to a professional relationship between psychotherapist and client having the intention of finding relief from psychological and emotional distress. The first identified form of psychotherapy was psychoanalysis (see note 2.). Theoretical disputes and developments regarding the nature of the psyche, aetiology of distress, modes of resolution and technique have generated a profession of some hundreds of different schools of thought and different approaches to clinical practice. The practice of psychotherapy is not restricted to medical professionals, training requirements vary enormously and regulatory control varies. In the UK

registration regulation is voluntary and the multitude of models and identifiers can make it difficult for prospective clients to understand where to seek reliable, experienced and effective help.

2. Sigmund Freud; 6th May, 1856 to 23rd September, 1939 was an Austrian neurologist who became known as the founding father of psychoanalysis. He was a prolific theorist, clinician and writer. The Psychopathology of Everyday Life (1901) is one of the key texts that laid the basis for the theory of psychoanalysis. Psychoanalysis is a clinical method for treating psychopathology through dialogue between a patient and analyst. The 'talking cure' requires free association (in which patients report their thoughts without reservation and in whichever order they spontaneously occur) and focuses its interpretations and interventions on an analysis of the transference (the process in which patients displace on to their analysts feelings derived from their childhood). Freud's redefinition of sexuality to include its infantile forms led him to formulate the Oedipus complex as the central tenet of psychoanalytical theory. His analysis of his own and his patients' dreams as wish-fulfilments provided him with models for the clinical analysis of symptom formation and the mechanisms of repression. He proposed the existence of unconscious mechanisms as an agency which disrupts conscious states of mind and viewed such mechanisms as central to understanding human motivation and emotional distress.

3. Paranoia is generally understood to refer to the feelings of an individual that coalesce around a profound and unshakable mistrust of others, of a belief in the hostile intention of others and a lack of belief that they are unable to protect themselves from these hostile intentions. In psychodynamic terms paranoia is believed to result from a person's own unconscious anger and hostility being projected into the world around them and thus being perceived as external and directed back towards themselves.

4. This term, perhaps cliché, now seems to be in general usage. I first encountered it when reading the work of Lucy LaFarge, Clinical Professor of Psychiatry, Weill Cornell Medical College and I am indebted to her for it.

5. For a simple and readable account of general defence mechanisms see: Joseph Burgo, (2012) Why Do I Do That?: Psychological Defence Mechanisms and the Hidden Ways They Shape Our Lives, New Rise Press.

NOTES AND FURTHER READING

Chapter Three
1. Socrates; c. 469BC-399 BC was a classical Greek philosopher. Credited as one of the founders of Western philosophy, Socrates has become renowned for his contribution to the field of ethics. Socrates lends his name to the concepts of Socratic irony and the Socratic Method.
2. Aristotle; 384BC-322BC was a Greek philosopher and polymath. Aristotle's writings were the first to create a comprehensive system of Western philosophy, encompassing ethics, aesthetics, logic, science, politics, and metaphysics. Together with Plato and Socrates, Aristotle is one of the most important founding figures in Western philosophy.
3. Sir Francis Bacon; 22nd January 1561 to 9th April 1626 was an English philosopher, statesman, scientist, jurist, orator and author. After his death, he remained extremely influential through his works, especially as philosophical advocate and practitioner of the scientific method during the scientific revolution. The quotation given here is from Bacon, F. (1597) Essays Civil and Moral, London, Ward, Lock and Co. Ltd.
4. Trudy Govier is an Associate Professor of Philosophy at the University of Lethbridge in Lethbridge, Alberta, Canada and has made an enormous contribution to establishing practical and sustainable models of conflict resolution.

Chapter Four
1. Neurosis is a catch-all description describing emotional responses that are not fully congruent with here and now experience. Whilst it can be shown that, to some degree, this applies to all emotional responses the term 'neurotic response' is generally reserved for those responses which, emanating from unresolved childhood distress, will disrupt present reality and disrupt, or make impossible, convivial and co-operative relationships.
2. Social theories are frameworks of empirical evidence used to study and interpret social phenomena. Social theory as a distinct discipline emerged in the 20th century and was largely equated with an attitude of critical thinking based on rationality, logic and objectivity, and the desire for knowledge through gathering empirical evidence rather than a priori methods.

3. The Frankfurt School was a school of neo-Marxist interdisciplinary social theorists and initially consisted of dissident Marxists who believed that some of Marx's followers had come to parrot a narrow selection of Marx's ideas, usually in defence of orthodox Communist parties. Critical of capitalism and Soviet socialism, their writings pointed to the possibility of an alternative path to social development.

4. Erich Fromm; March 23rd, 1900 to March 18th, 1980) was a German social psychologist, psychoanalyst, sociologist, humanistic philosopher, and democratic socialist. His works include Escape from Freedom (1941), The Art of Loving (1956) and To Have or To Be (1976).

5. Herbert Marcuse; July 19th, 1898 to July 29th, 1979) was a German philosopher, sociologist, and political theorist. His intellectual concerns were the dehumanizing effects of capitalism and modern technology. Celebrated as the "Father of the New Left" his best known works are Eros and Civilization (1955) and One-Dimensional Man (1964). His writings and Marxist scholarship have been the inspiration of many radical intellectuals and political activists.

6. Theodor W. Adorno; September 11th 1903 to August 6th, 1969 was a German sociologist, philosopher and musicologist known for his critical theory of society. He is widely regarded as one of the 20th century's foremost thinkers on aesthetics and philosophy and a critic of both fascism and what he called the culture industry. His writings, such as Dialectic of Enlightenment (1947), Minima Moralia (1951) and Negative Dialectics (1966) strongly influenced the European New Left.

7. Wilhelm Reich; March 24th, 1897 to November 3rd, 1957 was an Austrian psychoanalyst, a member of the second generation of psychoanalysts after Sigmund Freud, and one of the most radical figures in the history of psychiatry. He was the author of several influential books, most notably Character Analysis (1933), The Mass Psychology of Fascism (1933), and The Sexual Revolution (1936)

8. Marcuse (1955)

9. President John F Kennedy, from his Inaugural Address on January 20, 1961. The President presented the American public with a blueprint of his administration's foreign policy. The address typified Cold War thinking and characterised the Kennedy administration. It became known as the 'Kennedy doctrine'.

NOTES AND FURTHER READING

10. On the 3rd November, 1969, two weeks before the second massive Moratorium march on Washington, D.C., which attracted over 500,000 demonstrators against the war, President Richard Nixon made his celebrated speech on 'Vietnamisation.' He emphasised the necessity for the United States to achieve peace with honour and to avoid a sudden withdrawal. At the end of the speech, he called for the "great silent majority" to support him in this goal.

11. Martha Gellhorn; November 8th, 1908 to February 15th, 1998 was an American novelist, travel writer, and journalist, considered by the London Daily Telegraph, among others, to be one of the greatest war correspondents of the 20th century.

12. Gellhorn, M, (1959)

13. Anthony Blair; born 6 May 1953 is a British Labour Party politician who served as the Prime Minister of the United Kingdom from 1997 to 2007. The quotation is from 'Parkinson', a popular ITV chat show aired, 4th March, 2006.

14. Freud, S. (1929)

15. Lucy was discovered in 1974 by anthropologist Professor Donald Johanson and his student Tom Gray in a maze of ravines at Hadar in northern Ethiopia. Based on its small size, and pelvic shape, they concluded it was female and named it Lucy, after 'Lucy in the Sky with Diamonds', the Beatles song playing on the radio when Johanson and his team were celebrating the discovery.

16. Djilas, M (1958)

17. Milovan Đilas; June 4th, 1911 to April 20th, 1995 was a Yugoslav Communist politician, theorist and author. He was a key figure in the Partisan movement during World War II and in the post-war government. Đilas became one of the best-known and prominent dissidents in Yugoslavia and the whole of the Eastern Bloc.

Chapter Five

1. Stephen Jay Gould; September 10th, 1941 to May 20th, 2002 was an American palaeontologist, evolutionary biologist, and historian of science. He was also one of the most influential and widely read writers of popular science of his generation. Gould was known by the general public mainly from his 300 popular essays in the magazine Natural History. In April 2000, the US Library of Congress named him a 'Living Legend'.

NOTES AND FURTHER READING

2. Stephen Jay Gould, in conversation with Colin Tudge, BBC Radio 3, The Listener, September 20th, 1984, p. 19.
3. McGinn, C. (1989)
4. Darwin, C. (1859)
5. Charles Darwin, February 12th, 1809 to April 19th, 1882 was an English naturalist. He established that all species of life have descended over time from common ancestors and proposed the scientific theory that this branching pattern of evolution resulted from a process he called natural selection. According to the theory of natural selection, the random and objectiveless quest for existence has a similar effect to artificial selection involved in selective breeding. Darwinism originally included the broad concepts of transmutation of species that gained general scientific acceptance following the publication of 'On the Origin of Species'. Subsequently, the term refers to specific concepts of natural selection combined with later theories of genetics in molecular biology. Darwinism correctly refers only to biological evolution and the acceptance of Darwin's, and his successors, work in preference to other theories of life such as intelligent and divine design or extra-terrestrial origins.
6. Gregor Johann Mendel; July 20th, 1822 to January 6th, 1884 was a German-speaking Silesian scientist and Augustinian friar who gained posthumous fame as the founder of the new science of genetics. Mendel demonstrated that the inheritance of certain traits in pea plants follows particular patterns, now referred to as the laws of Mendelian inheritance. The profound significance of Mendel's work was not recognized until the turn of the 20th century, when the independent rediscovery of these laws initiated the modern science of genetics
7. Punctuated equilibrium is a theory in evolutionary biology that proposes most species will exhibit little net evolutionary change for most of their geological history, remaining in an extended state called stasis. When significant evolutionary change occurs, the theory proposes that it is generally restricted to rare and rapid events of branching speciation called cladogenesis. Cladogenesis is the process by which a species splits into two distinct species, rather than one species gradually transforming into another. In 1972, palaeontologists Niles Eldredge and Stephen Jay Gould published a landmark paper developing this theory and called it punctuated equilibria, in which they proposed that the degree of gradualism commonly attributed to

Charles Darwin is virtually non-existent in the fossil record, and that stasis dominates the history of most fossil species.

8. Evolvability is defined as the capacity of a system for adaptive evolution. Evolvability is the ability of a population of organisms not only to generate genetic diversity, but to generate adaptive genetic diversity, and thereby evolve more efficiently through natural selection.

9. Creationism is the religious belief that life, the Earth, and the universe are the creation of a supernatural being. As science developed during the 18th century and forward, various views aimed at reconciling science with the Abrahamic creation narrative developed in Western societies. Those holding that species had been created separately (such as Philip Gosse in 1847) were generally called 'advocates of creation' but were also called 'creationists'. As the creation vs. evolution controversy developed over time, the term 'anti-evolutionists' became common. In 1929, in the United States, the term 'creationism' first became associated with Christian fundamentalists, specifically with their rejection of human evolution and belief in a young Earth.

10. Steve Mithen is a Professor of Archaeology at the University of Reading. He has written a number of books including The Singing Neanderthals (2005) and The Prehistory of the Mind: The Cognitive Origins of Art, Religion and Science (1996).

11. Nicholas Humphrey is an English psychologist, based in Cambridge, who is known for his work on the evolution of human intelligence and consciousness. His books include A History of the Mind (1992) and Soul Dust: the Magic of Consciousness (2012).

Chapter Six

1. An 'emotion' is a biochemical response to a specific stimulus causing a change in the body's chemical profile and thereby changes in the cells and tissues of the body. It may simultaneously be defined by changes in the neural structures, which themselves have initiated the change in chemical profile, and each may progress in reverberation with each other. The 'feeling' of the emotion is the sensory representation of that change in neural patterns. The resultant sensations and cognitive images being simultaneously accompanied by a sense of knowing, generated though the state of consciousness of the self. Thus, the feeling of an emotion is a combination of sensory acuity together with a cognitively induced personal narrative meaning.

2. For a more detailed and highly engaging account of this view of the function of emotion, see Antonio Damasio's excellent book, The Feeling of What Happens (2000)
3. Low level, chronic symptoms of non-specific trauma are extremely common and a general hyper-sensitivity is the core component of such symptoms. The person will be 'jumpy', emotionally labile and may be intolerant of noise and sensory stimulation to a degree that they avoid these things where possible. Where it cannot be avoided, the person may start to feel quickly overwhelmed, unable to think straight and commonly display extreme irritation and sometimes, violence. At such times they will usually seek solitude and yet, at the same time, experience profound loneliness and helplessness.
4. Jacques Monod; February 9th, 1910 to May 31st, 1976 was a French biologist and was awarded a Nobel Prize in Physiology or Medicine in 1965. He was also a fine musician and esteemed writer on the philosophy of science.
5. Monod, J. (1971)
6. Margulis, L. (1998)

Chapter Seven
1. Camus, A. (1942)
2. Stolorow, R.D. (1986)
3. Krystal, H. (1978)
4. The 'given's' are described as a fundamental concern within existential schools of psychotherapy. Existential psychotherapy draws its basic assumptions from Existential Philosophy, a philosophical movement originated in Europe in the 19th century in the works of Kierkegaard, Nietzsche, Husserl, Heidegger and Sartre. Central to this movement is existence and what it means to be human in a world devoid of intrinsic meaning and subject to random occurrences. Generally identified as a group of 4 or 5 essential facts, the givens can also refer to any event impacting on our lives. The givens are not, of themselves, right or wrong but result in emotional struggles for the individual concerned. Martin Heidegger; September 26th, 1889 to May 26th, 1976, wrote that we are 'thrown into the world'. We have then to deal with whatever existence randomly throws at us.
5. Carl Jung; July 26th, 1875 to June 6th, 1961 was a Swiss psychiatrist and psychotherapist who founded analytical psychology. His work has been influential in psychiatry and in the study of religion, literature, and

related fields. The central concept of analytical psychology is individuation – the psychological process of integrating the opposites, including the conscious with the unconscious, while still maintaining their relative autonomy. Jung considered individuation to be the central process of human development.

6. Ernest Becker; September 27th, 1924 to March 6th, 1974 was a cultural anthropologist and interdisciplinary scientific thinker and writer. He is noted for his 1974 Pulitzer Prize-winning book, The Denial of Death.

7. Becker, E. (1973)

Chapter Eight

1. T. S. Eliot; September 26th, 1888 to January 4th, 1965 was a publisher, playwright, literary and social critic and widely regarded as one of the twentieth century's major poets. Eliot attracted widespread attention for his poem The Love Song of J. Alfred Prufrock (1915) is seen as a masterpiece of the Modernist movement. It was followed by some of the best-known poems in the English language, including The Waste Land (1922) and Four Quartets (1945). He is also known for his seven plays, particularly Murder in the Cathedral (1935) and was awarded the Nobel Prize in Literature in 1948. The Cocktail Party was written and first performed in 1949.

2. Eliot, T.S. (1949)

3. Samuel Langhorne Clemens; November 30th, 1835 to April 21st, 1910 was known by his pen name Mark Twain, was an American author and humourist. He wrote The Adventures of Tom Sawyer (1876) and its sequel, Adventures of Huckleberry Finn (1885). His wit and satire, in prose and in speech, earned praise from critics and peers and he was a friend to presidents, artists, industrialists, and European royalty.

4. Shirley Jackson; December 14th, 1916 to August 8th, 1965 was an American author. A popular writer in her time and her work has received increasing attention from literary critics in recent years. She is best known for the short story, The Lottery (1948), portraying a secret and sinister underside to bucolic small-town America. She is also well known for the 1959 novel The Haunting of Hill House, which was adapted in the 1963 film, The Haunting.

5. Narcissism is a natural consequence of normal human psychological development and is tempered through development by empathy,

gratitude and regard for others as separate people with rights and needs of their own. However, in unmodified or extreme cases, and except in the sense of primary narcissism or healthy self-regard or self-love, narcissism can usually be shown to be disruptive to in a person or group's relationships with self and others. It can be defined as an unhelpful concern with an image of the self to the exclusion, or distortion, of consensual reality.

6. See note 2., Chapter 2.

7. Otto Rank; April 22nd, 1884 to October 31st, 1939 was an Austrian psychoanalyst, writer, and teacher. He was one of Sigmund Freud's closest colleagues for 20 years. In 1926, following disputes with Freud's inner circle for his de-emphasis of the oedipal scenario and his increasing emphasis on the real, here and now relationship between mother and child, Otto Rank left Vienna for Paris and had a successful career as a lecturer, writer and therapist in France and then, after 1935 in the United States. Rank was highly influential in developing a more active and egalitarian psychotherapy focused on the here-and-now, real relationship, conscious mind and will, in contrast to a focus on early life, transference and the vicissitudes of the unconscious. His influence as an innovator in interpersonal and existential psychotherapy is generally understated as he is a link person towards object relations theory and practice. His highly engaging writings are full of insights on art, myth, religion, education, will, soul, life-fear and death-fear, and the 'art' of psychotherapy.

8. Freud, S. (1914)

9. Rank, O. (1911)

10. Freud, S. (1914)

11. Heinz Kohut; May 3rd, 1913 to October 8th, 1981 was an Austrian-born, American psychoanalyst best known for the development of Self Psychology that highlights the importance of relationship with others in the creation of self-esteem and well-being. In contrast to traditional psychoanalysis, Self-Psychology places a great deal of emphasis on the vicissitudes of real relationships. Kohut's essential view of narcissism is that, by creating an acceptable, though illusory, image of themselves the person can eliminate their sense of worthlessness.

12. Unmodified narcissism might be seen as instrumentally wrong in that it provokes as many problems as it solves. However, given that narcissism owes its development to childhood, a time of life where real emotional choices are severely restricted, it can be argued that the

narcissistic compromise is a psychologically effective manoeuvre and therefore correct in the circumstances.

13. Paranoia is a thought process emanating from anxiety and involves degrees of irrationality and delusion. It typically includes persecutory beliefs, feelings of danger and hostility. The sufferer experiences both generalised and specific feelings of dread and threats to their safety. In psychodynamic theory, paranoia is generally regarded as being a projection of a person's own disowned hostility, violence and rage into the world, thus rendering the world a place full of hostility, violence and rage.

Chapter Nine

1. Psychological omnipotence is the feeling of being all knowing, all powerful, and irresistible in your desires. This may occur as episodic flashes in everyday life at moments of emotional intensity but can be of clinical significance when associated with chronic narcissistic states. Omnipotence is generally regarded as healthy in infancy and as a precursor to reality based self-esteem. The successful transition from one to the other is one of the most crucial psychological milestones in child development.

2. Psychological introjection is the result of internalising aspects of another person's values or beliefs in such a way that they come to feel as if they are our own values and beliefs. This can be advantageous, if the introject is loving, supportive and benign or disabling if the introject is hateful, destructive and malignant. Introjection occurs as an emotional imperative and is motivated either by a wish to identify with a pleasing quality or of not identifying with a threatening quality in those around us.

3. Psychological projection was conceptualized by Sigmund Freud in the 1890s as a defence mechanism in which a person unconsciously rejects his or her own unacceptable attributes and ascribes them to other people. Although generally viewed as an immature defence the projection of one's negative qualities onto others is a common process in everyday life and the core component in the development of prejudice and scapegoating.

4. Melanie Klein; March 30th, 1882 to September 22nd, 1960 was an Austrian-born, British psychoanalyst and developed analytic techniques to use with children as young as 2 years old. Her understanding of the child's deepest fears and its defences against

them, enabled her to make a unique theoretical contributions to psychoanalysis, most notably the 'paranoid-schizoid position' and the 'depressive position'. Additionally her work had a significant impact on developmental psychology and her play therapy technique is still widely used today. Notable works include, Envy and Gratitude and other Works, 1946-1963 (1984), Love, Guilt and Reparation (1984) and The Psycho-Analysis of Children (1984).

5. Repetition compulsion is a psychological phenomenon in which a person repeats, or causes to be repeated, difficult, distressing or traumatic events. The purpose of such behaviour is twofold: repetitions of events in the hope or expectation of achieving a belated mastery of those events (a happy ending rather than an unhappy one) and: repetitions due to the need of the interrupted emotional process to find a resolution. Careful analysis and reflection upon repetition compulsion is essential in understanding the aetiology of adult distress. In psychotherapeutic technique the analysis and understanding of repetition that takes place in the consulting room, known as the transference, is the key therapeutic tool.

6. Arthur Hyatt-Williams; September 23rd, 1914 to August 27th, 2009 was a pioneering psychiatrist and psychoanalyst. He believed strongly that even the most hardened criminals, including murderers for whom there was no chance of direct reparation, could be helped to work on their sense of guilt and modify their destructive tendencies. His work and theoretical orientation is impressively detailed in his best known work, Cruelty, Violence and Murder, Understanding the Criminal Mind, (1998).

7. Hyatt-Williams, A. (1998)

8. Wilfred Bion; September 8th, 1897 to November 8th, 1979 was a British psychoanalyst and has been described as the greatest psychoanalytical thinker since Freud. He is best known for work stemming from his psychoanalysis of patients in psychotic states and for building on and expanding Klein's concepts of projective identification and the paranoid-schizoid and depressive positions. His best known works include: Experiences in Groups, and other Papers (1998) and Learning from Experience (1984).

9. Bion, W. (1959), (1962)

10. Shakespeare (1602)

11. Shakespeare, W. (1597)

12. LaFarge, L. (2006)

NOTES AND FURTHER READING

13. Shakespeare (1603)
14. Kohut, H. (1972)
15. Fatal Attraction is a 1987 American psychological thriller concerning a married man who has a weekend affair with a woman who then refuses to allow the affair to end, resulting in emotional blackmail, stalking, and an enduring obsession to revenge on her part. Sleeping with the Enemy is a 1991 psychological thriller about a woman who fakes her own death to escape from an abusive, obsessive husband who than discovers her deception and pursues her in revenge. The Hand That Rocks the Cradle is a 1992 American psychological thriller about a wronged and vengeful nanny out to destroy a naïve woman and steal her family.
16. Attachment disorder is a broad term intended to describe disorders of mood, behaviour and social relationships resulting from a failure to form normal attachments to primary care giving figures in childhood. Such a failure would result from early experiences of neglect, abuse or separation from caregivers between the ages of 6 months and 3 years.
17. William Ronald Fairbairn; August 11th, 1889 to December 31st, 1964 was a Scottish psychiatrist and psychoanalyst and a central figure in the development of the object relations theory of psychoanalysis. Building on the work of Melanie Klein, but in contrast to traditional psychoanalysis, his theory and practice was more concerned with the relationships between people than with the drives within them. His best known works are Psychoanalytical Studies of the Personality (1952) and From Instinct to Self: Selected Papers of W. R. D. Fairbairn (1994)
18. Attachment theory describes the dynamics of long-term relationships between humans. Its most important tenet is that an infant needs to develop a relationship with at least one primary caregiver for social and emotional development to occur normally. Attachment theory is an interdisciplinary study encompassing the fields of psychological, evolutionary, and ethological theory and has had far reaching influences on social policy in respect of child care and education.

Chapter Ten
1. See note 4, chapter 9.
2. See note 8, chapter 9.

3. Hanna Segal; August 20th, 1918 to July 5th, 2011 was a Polish born, British psychoanalyst and a follower of Melanie Klein. An innovative and talented clinician in her own right she is also widely credited with bringing Klein's work to the prominence it enjoys today. Her 1964 Introduction to the Work of Melanie Klein remains the most accessible overview of Klein's work. Segal's own works include The Work of Hanna Segal: Delusion and Artistic Creativity and other Psychoanalytic Essays (1986) and Psychoanalysis, Literature and War (1997).
4. See note 17, chapter 9.
5. Donald Winnicott; April 7th, 1896 to January 28th, 1971 was an English paediatrician and psychoanalyst. His work with children and their mothers informed the experience on which he built his most influential concepts, such as the 'holding environment' and the 'transitional object.' He also introduced the influential idea, and a detailed conceptualisation, of the true self and false self. His books include The Child and the Family (1957) and Playing and Reality (1971).
6. Depressive anxieties can be distinguished from the earlier paranoid anxieties by their preoccupation with the realisation of a capacity to harm or drive away a person whom the individual ambivalently loves. In accommodating and working through depressive anxiety, projections are withdrawn, ambivalence is tolerated and the other person is allowed more autonomy, reality, and a separate existence. It is anxiety consequent upon a realisation of the facts of life, similar to that revealed in existential theories of the person.
7. Klein, M. (1940)
8. The death of primitive narcissism or, at least, its redundancy.

Chapter Eleven
1. The Chiron Centre for Body Psychotherapy was a training and accreditation centre located in Ealing, West London. The centre was originally set up in 1983 by Bernd Eiden, Jochen Lude and Rainer Pervöltz. It closed in July 2010. The work of the Centre was instrumental in developing a unique form of integrated, relational body psychotherapy.
2. Body Psychotherapy is a model of psychotherapeutic thinking and intervention that places the somatic experience at the centre of the genesis of the self. Further, it supposes that somatic experience, and reflection on that experience, provides the starting point of therapeutic

NOTES AND FURTHER READING

intervention and change. Further information on Body Psychotherapy in the United Kingdom can be found at the Chiron Association for Body Psychotherapists: www.body-psychotherapy.org.uk

3. The autonomic nervous system (ANS or visceral nervous system or involuntary nervous system) is the part of the nervous system that acts as a control system, functioning largely below the level of consciousness, and controls visceral functions. The ANS affects all the systems of the body and will automatically adapt the body to deal with prevailing conditions. It is self-regulatory and intimately connected with emotional states. The ANS is central to the body's response to threat and will respond to physical. Emotional and imaginary threats. When the person feels themselves to be threatened in some way, part of the ANS will act to prepare the body for action – this will be the familiar fight or flight response but can also help with displays of counter-threat in order to avoid fight or flight (posturing) and sometimes a freezing of the body's responses. ANS responses are commonly visible to the observant therapist and will provide information about the state of arousal, or otherwise, of the client. This information can then be used to help the therapist when making effective therapeutic interventions.

Bibliography

Adorno, T.W. (1947) Dialectic of Enlightenment, Verso Books; New Ed edition 1997.
Adorno, T.W. (1951) Minima Moralia, Verso Books; New Ed edition 2005.
Adorno, T.W. (1966) Negative Dialectics, Routledge and Keegan Paul 1973.
Becker, E. 1973, The Denial of Death, Simon and Schuster.
Bion, W. (1998) Experiences in Groups and Other Papers, Routledge.
Bion, W. (1984) Learning from Experience, Karnac.
Bion, W. (1959) Attacks on Linking, International Journal of Psychoanalysis, 40: 308-15.
Bion, W. (1962) Theory of Thinking, International Journal of Psychoanalysis, 43: 306-10.
Bronte, E. (1847) Wuthering Heights, Wordsworth Classics, reprint 1992.
Burgo, J. (2012) Why Do I Do That?: Psychological Defense Mechanisms and the Hidden Ways They Shape Our Lives, New Rise Press.
Camus, A. (1942) The Myth of Sisyphus, Penguin, 2005.
Damasio, A. (2000) The Feeling of What Happens, Vintage.
Darwin, C. (1859) The Origin of Species, Wordsworth Classics, 1998.
Dickens, C. (1838) Oliver Twist, Wordsworth Classics, reprint 2011.
Djilas, M (1958) Land Without Justice, London, Harcourt Brace.
Eldredge, Niles and S. J. Gould (1972) Punctuated equilibria: an alternative to phyletic gradualism, in T.J.M. Schopf, ed., Models in Paleobiology, San Francisco: Freeman Cooper. pp. 82-115.
Eliot, T.S. (1950) The Cocktail Party, Harcourt Brace.
Fairbairn, W.R.D. (1952) Psychoanalytical Studies of the Personality, Psychology Press.
Fairbairn, W.R.D. (1994) From Instinct to Self: Selected Papers of W. R. D. Fairbairn, Jason Aronson Inc.
Freud, S. (1914) On Narcissism, S.E., X, 141. The Standard Edition of the Complete Psychological Works of Sigmund Freud, James Strachey, London, 1953-73.
Freud, S. (1929) Civilization and Its Discontents, Penguin, reprint 2002
Fromm, E. (1941) Escape from Freedom, Farrar and Rinehart.
Fromm, E. (1976) To Have or To Be, Harper and Row.

BIBLIOGRAPHY

Fromm, E. (1956) The Art of Loving, Continuum International.

Gellhorn, M, (1959) The Face of War, updated in 1986, Atlantic Monthly Press, reprint 1994

Govier, T. (2002) Forgiveness and Revenge, London, Routledge.

Humphrey, N. (1992) A History of the Mind, Simon and Schuster.

Humphrey, N. (2012) Soul Dust: the Magic of Consciousness, Quercus.

Hyatt-Williams, A. (1998) Cruelty, Violence and Murder, Understanding the Criminal Mind, Karnac Books.

Klein, M. (1940) Mourning and its Relation to Manic-Depressive States, The International Journal of Psychoanalysis 21, 125-153.

Klein, M. (1984) Envy and Gratitude and Other Works 1946-1963, Free Press

Klein, M. (1984) Love, Guilt and Reparation and Other Works 1921-1945, Free Press

Klein, M. (1984) The Psycho-Analysis of Children, Free Press

Kohut, H. (1972) Thoughts on Narcissism and Narcissistic Rage, Psychoanalytic Study of the Child, 27: 360-400.

Krystal, H. (1978) Trauma and Affects, Psychoanalytical Study of the Child, Yale University Press, Vol. 38.

LaFarge, L. (2006) The Wish for Revenge, Psychoanalytic Quarterly, 75 (2), 447-475.

Margulis, L. (1998) The Symbiotic Planet: A New Look at Evolution, Weidenfield and Nicolson.

Marcuse, H. (1955) Eros and Civilisation, Beacon Press; 8th edition 1974.

Marcuse, H. (1964) One-Dimensional Man, Beacon Press; 2 edition 1991.

McGinn, C. (1989) Can We Solve the Mind-Body Problem? Mind 98, 349-66

Middleton, T. & Rowley, W. (1653) The Changeling, in Three Revenge Tragedies, Penguin Books, pp. 259-343

Mithen, S. (2005) The Singing Neanderthals, London: Weidenfeld and Nicolson.

Mithen, S. (1996) The Prehistory of the Mind: The Cognitive Origins of Art, Religion and Science, Thames and Hudson.

Monod, J. (1971) Chance and Necessity, London, Collins.

Rank, O. (1911) A Contribution to Narcissism, Annals of Psychoanalytic and Psychopathological Research, F. Deuticke

Reich, W. (1933) Character Analysis, Farrar, Straus and Giroux 1980.
Reich, W. (1933) The Mass Psychology of Fascism, Harmondsworth 1975.
Reich, W. (1936) The Sexual Revolution, Macmillan, 2013
Segal, H. (1964) Introduction to the Work of Melanie Klein, Heinemann; republished by Hogarth Press.
Segal, H. (1986) The Work of Hanna Segal: Delusion and Artistic Creativity and other Psycho-analytic Essays, Free Association Books.
Segal, H. (1997) Psychoanalysis, Literature and War, Routledge.
Shakespeare, W. (1597) Romeo and Juliet, in the Complete Works of William Shakespeare, Magpie Books, 1993.
Shakespeare, W. (1602) Hamlet, Prince of Denmark, in the Complete Works of William Shakespeare, Magpie Books, 1993.
Shakespeare, W. (1603) Othello, in the Complete Works of William Shakespeare, Magpie Books, 1993.
Steadman, Ralph. (2016) Interview with Xan Rice, *The New Statesman*, December, 2016
Stolorow, R.D. (1986) Critical Reflections on the Theory of Self-Psychology: an Inside View, Psychoanalytic Inquiry, Analytic Press, Vol. 6.
Tolstoy, L. (1877) Anna Karenina, Penguin Classics, reprint 2003.
Tourneur, C. (1606) The Revenger's Tragedy, in Three Revenge Tragedies, Penguin Books, pp. 40-136.
Webster, J. (1612) The White Devil, in Three Revenge Tragedies, Penguin Books, pp. 137-258.
Winnicott, D. (1957) The Child and the Family, Perseus Books Group.
Winnicott, D. (1971) Playing and Reality, Tavistock Publications.

INDEX

Act of Will, 41
Amoebae, 73
Anxiety, 86, 92
Aristotle, 38
Art, 76
Attachment Disorder, 134
Attachment Theory, 135-6
Autonomic Nervous System, 159

Bacon, Francis, 38
Becker, Ernest, 99
Bion, Wilfred, 124, 140
Blair, Anthony, 51
Body Psychotherapy, 158

Children's Revenge Game, 33
Conflict Resolution, 25, 93
Cowardice, 64, 96

Darwin, Charles, 66-7
Death, 98
Defence Strategies, 28-29
Denial of Feeling, 9-10
Depressive Anxiety, 145
Depressive Position, 141-2
Desexualisation, 48
Deterrence, 37, 90, 93
Dilas, Milovan, 56, 58
Disillusion, 103-5
Divorce, 1, 19, 23-6
Drives and Instincts, 93-4

Ego, 94
Eliot, Thomas Sterns, 103, 105, 131
Embodied Sensation, 62

Emotion
   and reality, 101
   definition, 77-9, 80-2
   narrative meaning, 77-9
   regulatory function, 78-9
   sensory content, 79
Emotional Residue, ii
Envy, 126-7, 143
Erich Fromm, 47-8
Evolution, 66-70
   altruism, 66
   evolvability, 67
   of the brain, 70
   punctuated equilibrium, 67
   self-consciousness, 70-6
Existential Psychotherapy, 95
   givens, 97
Exteroception, 61

Fairbairn, Ronald, 135, 140
Fairness, feelings of, 24-5
Family Lawyers, 26, 26
Fatal Attraction (film), 133
Forgiveness, 40-2
Frankfurt School, 47
Freud, Sigmund, 46-8, 52, 93, 106, 109-10, 116
Fundamentalism, 116

Gellhorn, Martha, 51
Getting Away With It, 4, 63, 156-7
Gould, Stephen Jay, 65
Grief, 2, 6, 10, 26, 107, 128, 136

Hamlet, 124, 128

INDEX

Hatred, 5-9, 24, 39, 56, 94, 117, 126, 130, 151, 159
Head and Belly, 8, 85
Herbert Marcuse, 47-48
Homeostasis, 86
Homo Erectus, 53
Homo Sapiens, 36, 54-5
Honour, 13, 57-8
Humphrey, Nicolas, 69
Hyatt-Williams, Arthur, 123

Injunction, 47
Instinct, 68, 93
Institute for Social Research, 47
Intelligence 70-9
   figurative thought, 71
   integration, 71
   musical analogy, 72
   situation specific, 70
Interoception, 61-2, 73
Introject, 121-2, 177
Isolation, 2, 79, 89, 98, 103, 177

Jackson, Shirley, 105
Jung, Carl, 99
Justice, 2, 79, 89, 98, 103, 177

Kennedy, John F, 50
King, Martin Luther, 50
Klein, Melanie, 122, 126-7, 140, 144
Kohut, Heinz, 110, 133
Krystal, Henry, 94

LaFarge, Lucy, 129
Lee, Robert E, 50

Meaninglessness, 99. 105.133
Mediation, 5, 75
Mendel, Gregor, 66
Middleton, Thomas, 125
Mithen, Stephen, 69
Monod, Jacques, 88-9, 95
Moral Ambivalence, 42
Mother Teresa, 50
Mourning, 128, 136-7, 141-2, 153-5, 158,

Narcissism, 106-11
   and arrogance, 113
   and parenting, 114
   and regression, 113
   and violence, 114
   primary, 109-10
   rage, 122, 130, 133, 149
Narcissistic Mortification, 144, 155-7
Narcissus, 107-8
Nemesis, goddess, 108
Neurosis, 46-7, 84, 86-7, 106, 160
Neurotic Compromise, 64
Nixon, Richard, 51
Non-Combatants, 51

Object Relations, 140
Objects, good and bad, 126, 140-1
Oliver Twist, 11
Omnipotence, 66, 110, 112, 114, 120, 124, 132, 137, 151
Operational Consciousness, 70
Organic Basis of Selfhood, 68, 72-3, 75
Origin of the Species, 66

INDEX

Othello, 131

Paranoia, 115, 130, 134, 145
Paranoid-Schizoid Position, 141
Payback, 9, 139, 158
Potency, 55-6, 60, 110, 120-1, 129-30
Prejudice, 29, 114, 123, 164
Proprioception, 61-2, 73
Psychological Manoeuvre, 4-9, 16, 22, 28, 31
Psychotherapy, 21, 106, 144, 145

Rank, Otto, 106
Rape, 128
Reality Principle, 48
Repetition Compulsion, 122, 134
Responsibility, 97
Retaliation, 35-7
Revenge
  addictive, 132
  attachment, 129
  backward orientation, 38-9
  economic stability, 35
  ethical disapproval of, 38-40
  illusion, 25-6
  irrational act, 9, 31, 38
  joy of, 8, 56-7
  passive, 4, 84, 123
  psychological objection, 118
  instrumental error, 23-4, 91, 118-9
Revenge Scenario, ii, 5-6, 11, 22, 30, 35, 118, 120
Romeo and Juliet, 99, 128

Sartre, John-Paul, 96
Scapegoat, 5, 29, 34, 123
Segal, Hannah, 140
Self-Esteem, definition, 60-3
Self-Esteem, development, 61
Self-significance, 55-8, 61
Serial Killer, 62
Shakespeare, William, 125, 128, 131
Sleeping with the Enemy (film), 133
Social Theory, 46-7
Socrates, 38
Steadman, Ralph, 45
Stimulus and Response, 65, 68, 73-6
Stolorow, Robert, 94
Story Telling, 99-100, 104-5, 114
Suicide, 108, 147
Surplus Repression, 47-8

The Hand that Rocks the Cradle (film), 133
Theodore Adorno, 47-8
The Revenger's Tragedy, 125
Tolstoy, Leo, 1
Tourneur, Cyril, 125, 131
Trudy Govier, 40
Twain, Mark, 105

Unfinished Business, 14, 134

Vendetta, 30, 39, 57, 69, 147
Vietnam War, 50-1
Violence
  and civilisation, 43
  apocalyptic, 56

    archaeological evidence, 53-4
    comfort, 45
    definition, 44
    global poverty, 52
Violent Evacuation, 124

Walt Disney, 92
War, 49-50
Water into Wine, 65
Webster, John, 125
Wilhelm Reich, 47-8
Winnicot, Donald, 140
World Health Organisation, 51
Wrongdoing
    ethical, 19
    instrumental, 19
    moral, 16
Wuthering Heights, 14

Yugoslavia, 57, 138

Zero-Sum Game, 35, 55, 109

Printed in Great Britain
by Amazon